Evelyn C. Hausknecht

UNSEEN ARMS
A STORY ABOUT CANCER, CRISIS,
AND BEING CARRIED BY FAITH

www.mascotbooks.com

Unseen Arms: A Story about Cancer, Crisis, and Being Carried by Faith

I have tried to recreate events, locales, and conversations from my memories of them. In order to maintain their anonymity in some instances I have changed the names of individuals and places. I may have changed some identifying characteristics and details such as physical properties, occupations, and places of residence.

For more information, please contact:
Mascot Books
620 Herndon Parkway, Suite 320
Herndon, VA 20170
info@mascotbooks.com

Library of Congress Control Number: 2021914563

CPSIA Code: PRV1221A
ISBN-13: 978-1-64543-922-6

Printed in the United States

Unseen Arms is dedicated to God our Father, Jesus our Savior, and Holy Spirit our Comforter. In addition, we dedicate this book to our family and friends who love us and continue to support us. The amazing medical community at Roswell Park Cancer Center in Buffalo, New York, and many other hospitals and medical personnel in every state where I have sought help have our great respect and appreciation. And last, but not least, we dedicate this book to the lively young custodian who took time to visit with me on those long, lonely nights at Roswell Park. I don't remember your name, but I remember your spirit. Thanks to all who helped me on this journey.

UNSEEN ARMS

A Story about Cancer, Crisis, and Being Carried by Faith

EVELYN & WAYNE HAUSKNECHT

CONTENTS

PROLOGUE
June 2006: A Trek Westward

In July 2006, Wayne and I went on the trip of our lives. We loaded our 2006 Harley Road King and headed west. About 7:30 a.m., we left home and stopped at McDonald's for a breakfast sandwich. We were both very excited, as neither of us had ridden our motorcycle for a long distance. Since we had purchased the motorcycle in the early spring, we had taken only one practice ride to visit our daughter, Kelly, in Carlisle, Pennsylvania.

The night before we left for Kelly's house, we'd towed the motorcycle from our house in Eaton, New York, to Wayne's mother's home in northern Pennsylvania. We spent the night with her and awoke the next morning to a drizzle and a foggy sky. We lingered over breakfast and hoped for the weather to clear. Later, the sky was brighter, but it was still drizzling. We decided it was time to go and climbed on the bike. We had a large luggage bag tied on the bike, along with a small, cylindrical bag for our toiletries, attached by zipper. Being dressed in leather jackets and chaps, along with boots, helped us keep the cold out and keep us safe. Wayne's mom peered out the window, and I was sure she thought we were crazy. After spending the night with Kelly and her family, we rode further south to our son's home in Virginia.

The practice trip went smoothly. Later in July, we towed the bike to Sioux Falls, South Dakota. The day before arriving there, we had crossed the Missouri River and realized that we were over a thousand miles from home. We were well on our way to our destination, where we would leave the truck and trailer and continue west on the motorcycle. Everywhere we stopped, bikers would ask us if we were on our way to Sturgis for bike week. I had no desire to go to Sturgis during bike week, because I had heard of the wildness that went on during that time. We did end up going through Sturgis, but it was the week before bike week, and the town was dead.

On July 10, the excitement mounted as we left the truck and trailer at the airport in Sioux Falls, South Dakota. A person at the motel where we stayed told Wayne to call Elvis at the airport to ask about a place to store our truck and trailer. Wayne was pleased that he could park inside a fenced area for twenty-four dollars per week. Finding a place to leave the truck and trailer was one of my concerns before we left home, but Wayne was not worried about finding a place. God had preplanned this trip for us, and all the details worked out as if we'd had a tour guide scheduling the trip. We did, in fact, have a guide—a supernatural guide!

On I-90 in Kimball, South Dakota, we stopped at the Doo-Wah Ditty's Diner for lunch. This café was styled like a '50s diner, and the menu was unique. I ordered a chili burger and was surprised that it was a hamburger floating in a large bowl of chili smothered with cheese. When we finished lunch, Wayne noticed there was a small tractor museum across the interstate. We decided to stop there for a visit. Inside, there were two elderly ladies, and one of them, an eighty-two-year-old widow, became our tour guide. Since I am not particularly interested in tractors, I was able to focus on the stories she shared.

Wayne enjoyed looking at the numerous tractors stored in two large metal sheds. It was a hot day with a temperature of over one hundred degrees. She told us about the windmills and earning her "walking about money" as a little girl by climbing the windmills and greasing the gears.

The other lady, who was in her nineties, was very interested in our motorcycle. She said that she had never ridden on a motorcycle and that she had always wanted to ride one. Wayne promised her he would give her a ride. Sadly, after we finished the tour, we forgot about her ride. Wayne remembered later in the day and felt bad that he had forgotten. As I said before, the tractors did not make an impression on me, but talking with the sweet old ladies was precious. The museum was not air-conditioned, but the ladies dressed in their print dresses did not seem to notice the heat. I noticed and was glad to get back onto the motorcycle, where I could feel the wind blowing across my face. One of the greatest joys of our trip was the wonderful people we met at all of our stops. They were interested in us and our journeys and glad to share about their lives.

There was not a lot of traffic along I-90 until we neared a city. I found it very interesting that once we pulled off the main highway all of the roads were gravel, and the towns were tiny.

It was ninety-two degrees when we crossed into the Crow Creek Indian Reservation. We continued to follow the Missouri River and took a scenic route northwest to Pierre, North Dakota. We were impressed with the beauty of the architecture of the state capitol.

The next day, we headed to Rapid City, South Dakota. Along the way, we drove through the Badlands. We were not prepared for the extreme heat. The leather jackets came off. The colors and shapes of the land were phenomenal. We stayed there for only a short time because of the high heat, rattlesnake warnings, lack of water, and distance we still needed to cover before nightfall. We met a man riding a tricycle, and he offered to take our picture.

Along the interstate, we kept seeing signs for "Wall Drug: Free Ice Water and 5 Cent Coffee." When we pulled up in front of Wall Drug, I felt like a cartoon, crawling out of the desert into the saloon in an old Western town. I was not sure I could walk when I got off the motorcycle. I was hot, thirsty, dusty, and tired, but I climbed off the motorcycle, entered the drug store, and headed straight for the ice water. Next, I found the ice cream, and after looking around and getting refreshed, we started the final stretch to Rapid City.

On July 12, we visited Mount Rushmore. There was a beautiful walk through the woods and over rocks at the bottom of the memorial. I had seen this monument in books and on TV but was not prepared for the visual impact of the monument up close. The details of the individual presidents' faces were impressive. The next day, we went back to the monument, walked up closer, and attended a lecture on how the measurements were scaled. We spent the afternoon sitting at the refreshment stand, just enjoying the soft breeze and the beauty around us. This allowed me the opportunity to mail some postcards home.

A few days later, we stopped in Cody, Wyoming. It was gorgeous and very hot that afternoon. We spent most of the afternoon visiting the air-conditioned Cody Firearm Museum in the Buffalo Bill Center of the West. Wayne enjoyed the seven thousand guns on display, and I enjoyed seeing the taxidermy of numerous large mammals.

After Cody, we rode across the Chief Joseph Scenic Byway to Cook City, Montana. This drive, along with the Bear Tooth Highway, was one of most exciting rides on which we ventured. High altitudes and switchbacks made this a biker's paradise, kept us on our toes, and kept Wayne's hand on the brakes. I screamed only once while we were going down into Cook City, when I thought Wayne was not braking fast enough. As usual, he had things under control. I was thankful to know who the real pilot was, and every time I felt afraid, I would look up to the heavens and pray. While in Cook City, we found a small outside restaurant where we ordered a hamburger. More than the burger, we enjoyed the majestic views and the interesting people in this small town overrun with people and motorcycles of every kind. One of the ladies dumped her bike while trying to park, and men from every direction appeared to help her right it. We also saw hundreds of motorcycles along these routes, and that pleased Wayne.

After that, we traveled from Billings to Butte, Montana. On July 17, we pulled into Whitefish, Montana, where we stayed two nights. On July 18, we had the biggest adventure of all at Glacier National Park. We sat by Lake McDonald, where I told Wayne, "If we were younger, we would not be going back East." He agreed. We had fallen in love with the beauty of the West. After a while, we decided to ascend to the top of the world on the Going-to-the-Sun Road. Beautiful views surrounded us on all sides as we drove up the steep incline to the top. On the top of the mountain, there was a rest area where we got off the bike, refreshed ourselves, and took a walk on the rock surfaces. We saw mothers with baby mountain goats, waterfalls, and glaciers. While walking along a trail, Wayne came face-to-face with a large, bighorn ram that was standing on a huge boulder about twenty-five feet away. He took a picture before the ram snorted, stomped his leg, and peed on the rock. I think he was saying that Wayne should stay out of his territory. After his display of superiority, he meandered down the other side of the mountain.

The ride home was uneventful. Staying at the same towns and motels took away some of the adventure, but by now we were ready to go home. Our plans were to go back again the next year for a longer period of time, but cancer intervened, and we haven't been able to return yet. We still have a dream to return.

I started this book with the highlights of our journey out West because it was three weeks of complete harmony, unity, and joy. No thunderstorm, harsh word, or grey sky visited us on our trip. I believe this trip was a gift from God to strengthen us for the long, treacherous road which was to follow the next twelve years. As I hung onto the back of that Harley, I felt a peace and a precious calmness that was from God. I spent much of the ride praying and worshiping God for the beauty around us and for his glorious provision for us on this trip. When I was afraid on those high mountains, sharp switchbacks, and swift declines, a voice said, "Look up!" I didn't know how many times I would need to look up in the months and years ahead when I would have to fight for my life.

PART I

June 2007: Diagnosis and Treatment

AT THE TIME OF DIAGNOSIS, I did not know that, with my type of non-Hodgkin's T-cell lymphoma, I had a survival rate of less than 1 percent. Even with the stem cell transplant which I had in 2008, my chances of survival increased only a small amount. After the transplant, there was only a 3 percent chance that I would live a year. The hematologist-oncologist whom I saw in Florida said I was the only survivor she had ever seen or heard about with this exact diagnosis. My hematologist-oncologist in Richmond said there was less than a handful who had survived this diagnosis. My attending doctor at Roswell Park Cancer Institute said I was the reason he had stopped giving the "death talk." I have met only one person with my exact diagnosis. She lives in Minnesota, and I became her peer mentor through the Leukemia and Lymphoma Society. This is why I know I am a miracle and that by the grace of God I am a survivor.

Since May 2007, my life has had two sharp divisions: BC (before cancer) and AC (after cancer). Before cancer, my life was as normal as a life could be. I was an elementary school teacher with a husband and two adult children. Wayne and I had a son, Ben, and a daughter, Kelly. Ben and his wife, Yolanda, had a daughter, Anya, and a son, Sam. Kelly was married to John and had a daughter named Sophia. We also had a dog named Goldie and a cat named Grace.

Wayne and I lived in Eaton, which is in central New York. He was a professor at SUNY Morrisville College, and I taught fourth grade at Sherburne-Earlville Central School. We were Christians and sought God for his guidance and grace. We had ups and downs just like everyone else but had never dealt with a life-threatening disease.

On the Friday of the 2007 Memorial Day weekend, my husband called during my lunch period and asked me to call my family doctor. I responded that I would call at the end of the day. I did not want to call then because my students were in the cafeteria, and I needed to walk them back to class in a few minutes. Wayne insisted that I call since he knew it was very important and knew something was wrong. I had not been feeling well since October of 2006. I had seen my physician several times and had taken several tests to see what my problem was.

Finally, I agreed to call. I asked another teacher to walk my students to the classroom for me. She agreed, and I made a call to my family doctor in Hamilton. He told me he suspected I had cancer—lymphoma. He also told me this was his last day in this office because he was moving to Vermont that weekend. He had made an appointment for me to have a biopsy with a surgeon in Hamilton the next week to determine my exact diagnosis. In addition, he had made an appointment for me with a hematologist-oncologist in Cooperstown, New York, for the same week.

I called Wayne back to tell him I had talked with the doctor. I understood what the doctor said to me and understood the implication of his words, but I did not understand the seriousness or the deep truth of those words. Wayne, understanding the consequences much better than I, wanted to come to school to pick me up. I explained that I had only two more classes and that I would come home as soon as school was over. Wayne was determined to come get me. He said he did not want me to drive home. I could tell he was not trying to get me upset but that he was upset. I gave in and called the secretary and told her I needed to leave because I was sick. I did not want to toss the word *cancer* into the rumor mill until I was sure of the diagnosis. I gathered my things and waited until the aide came to cover my class. As soon as she arrived, I gave her brief instructions for the students to follow.

I left through a side door and waited near the parking lot. As I paced there for a while, the secretary came out to check on me. She probably wondered why I did not leave. I told her that I was waiting for Wayne to pick me up and that we would come back later to get my car. I convinced her I would be fine until Wayne came. She went back inside.

A few minutes later, the vice principal came out to talk to me. He kept me company, and we visited while I waited. Soon, I realized I had left my purse in the closet in my classroom. I asked him to go get it since I did not want to go back into the classroom with the students. By then, I think I was starting to understand what was going on. I did not want people to ask questions because I was close to tears. Soon after he returned with my purse, I saw Wayne's truck turn the corner. I told the VP thanks and went to get into the truck. As soon as I climbed in and saw the tears in Wayne's eyes, I knew this was a much more serious problem than I had imagined. We hugged and started home. We were both quiet, not really knowing what to say and trying to absorb the news.

About halfway home, a friend we often went out to dinner with called and asked if we wanted to meet for a fish dinner that night. I told her we couldn't go. That was the first time that I told someone that I might have cancer. I felt the tears developing and made the phone call brief. After that, we were in a state of shock, and I am not sure how we made it through the weekend. Wayne called Ben and Kelly and told them the diagnosis. Everyone was stunned and did not know what to say. Later, I called my mother and tried to explain to her something I did not understand myself. Wayne called his mother. One thing that made sharing this information difficult was that everyone asked questions to which we had no answers. I still did not believe I had cancer until the biopsy showed the exact diagnosis. In the meantime, I was tested for other issues.

The next week, I met with a surgeon in Hamilton, New York, where I was advised that I needed to have a lymph node removed from my right groin area so it could be tested to verify my diagnosis. It took about a week to get the test results. Wayne went with me to all the appointments and was a mountain of support. I later started to call him "Mr. Wonderful." He lived up to that name throughout the whole ordeal and continues to the present. By then, many people were praying for me, and that circle of prayer warriors grew larger as the journey continued.

Later that week, we went to see a hematologist-oncologist at Imogene Bassett Hospital in Cooperstown, New York. My first meeting with her was in early June, and I was frightened. I was about to jump headfirst into a medical pool that was unknown to either of us. I was overwhelmed and tired after driving the fifty-four miles from our home to Cooperstown. First, we had to wait in line and show my ID and insurance cards. Upon entering the waiting room, I sat in a corner not wanting to see anyone or be seen. Every patient in the waiting room looked to me like a victim of a great catastrophe. Many were bald with various types of hats, caps, and scarfs to cover their vulnerabilities. Wayne registered me, and then we sat quietly waiting to be called.

When it was our turn to swim through this question-infested water, we entered a small exam room where a nurse took my vitals and asked me questions. Soon the doctor entered the room and talked with us; we explained my symptoms over the last eight months. The doctor examined me, finding that my spleen was enlarged and that I had swollen lymphoma nodes the size of golf balls on the back of my head. She explained the numerous subtypes of lymphoma and informed me that I would need a bone marrow aspiration to determine how to stage the disease. A bone marrow aspiration requires that bone tissue be retrieved from your hip with a needle. The tissue is sent to a lab to determine the exact subtype of non-Hodgkin's lymphoma. I was taken to a room with a bed and told to lie on my stomach. After local anesthesia, the doctor proceeded to put the needle into my back at the top of my buttocks and withdraw bone tissue. It was very painful, but thankfully, the procedure took only a short time. I could not see the needle, but in my imagination, it was an enormously large, dull needle. I did not know I would have to have this procedure at least four more times. That procedure became my most dreaded and painful procedure in the medical arsenal of tests during the whole twelve years. However, having my tear ducts cauterized with a fiery needle was a close second. I am glad I did not know about many of the medical procedures I would endure.

At the next appointment, the doctor explained my diagnosis as an aggressive, recurrent type of non-Hodgkin's lymphoma and said that I might need a stem cell transplant. I was thinking I would need the transplant maybe ten years down the road, but Wayne understood that she meant soon.

A few days later, I saw the surgeon in Hamilton for his report on the lymph node biopsy. He told me that there was no sign of lymphoma. I interrupted him and told him I had already seen a hematologist-oncologist in Cooperstown. He said he would defer to her. Our visit with him was brief, and for the next biopsy, I saw a surgeon at Imogene Bassett Hospital in Cooperstown, New York.

The next week, I was at Cooperstown for my second appointment with the hematologist-oncologist and my first infusion of chemotherapy. The nurse took my vitals and asked me questions before I saw the doctor. The doctor then gave me another thorough examination. I had to have bloodwork before I could have the infusion. I didn't know that I was supposed to have my blood drawn from my fingertip, and the phlebotomist didn't know that I was there for an infusion.

Once I was approved to go ahead with the chemo, I went into the infusion room. It was a rectangular room with windows across one end. Recliners were lined up along the walls. Each chair had someone in it receiving chemo. Some patients were sleeping, some were reading, and others were talking quietly with someone who had brought them to the hospital. Each patient was allowed space to have one person stay with them.

When I got into my seat, my nurse, who was very nice, looked for a place to put the needle in my arm for the drug infusion. When she realized I had had blood drawn from my arm instead of my fingertip, she told me to never let the phlebotomist take blood from my arm again. She needed to have the blood draw below where she would put the needle for the infusion. I felt like she was yelling at me and began to cry silently. I was very vulnerable at that time. I thought I was not going to be able to get the infusion that day. I was scheduled to have six rounds of CHOP (a cocktail of chemo drugs) with a two-week rest period between the infusions. I like to think in terms of percentages and was telling myself that after this infusion, 16 percent of the procedures would be over. Wayne saw I was crying, and he asked me what was wrong. The nurse realized I was upset and began to apologize. She told me that I would be able to get the infusion that day, and I began to calm down.

While the chemist mixed the chemo drugs, the nurse started an infusion of a relaxation drug and a drip of Benadryl. The relaxation drug plus the Benadryl keep the patient from having side effects from the chemo. They made me sleepy. I turned to Wayne and told him I was going to sleep and that he did not need to stay. It was a lovely day outside, and Cooperstown is a tourist town with the National Baseball Hall of Fame and the Farmer's Museum along with a beautiful lake. After I was asleep and he knew I was not having any complications, he left for a walk. I think walking was one of the things that helped both of us keep our sanity while traveling this journey.

Each subsequent infusion was similar and started with a blood draw from the finger and a doctor visit. After the blood was processed, if the counts were high enough, I would begin the infusion. The pharmacists would not mix the chemo until they were assured the patient was strong enough to take the medicine. The medicines were so expensive and were mixed specially for each patient after the doctor visits. When I was receiving the chemo in 2007, the chemo cost ten thousand dollars per infusion.

The oncologist explained that I would lose my hair after the second infusion of chemo. She was accurate, and my hair started to come out in handfuls during my shower one morning. I have always worn my hair in a short style, but this looked like an enormous amount of hair. Now I had patches of baldness. Thankfully, Kelly, John, and Sophia were home that week for the July 4 celebrations in Hamilton, New York. My birthday was also that week, and we usually went to Hamilton for the parade and fireworks.

I was weak at the time, but I had planned for Kelly to take me to my hair stylist to have my head shaved. I was too weak to travel the long distance to Utica just to have my hair cut. I called my hair stylist, and she suggested we get a pair of clippers from the drugstore and have someone shave it at home. Kelly went to the drugstore and bought a pair of clippers. I asked Wayne to shave my head, but he said he could not do it. He offered to shave his for support, but I did not want him to shave his hair. It was important to me that one of us looked normal. Plus, I always liked his hair and did not want him to shave it. He had good intentions, and I appreciated his offer. I wanted the world around me to be as normal as it could be.

That left Kelly to do the job. We put a chair in the bathroom upstairs. I sat down, and she put a towel around my shoulders. Instead of shaving my head bald, we decided to cut it to the lowest setting on the clippers. I was surprised that neither of us cried, though we didn't talk. It was a solemn time for both of us. I sat with my own thoughts, and she buzzed and did the same. By that time, I cried easily, and we both knew that if we talked, we would cry, and that would make the job harder. It didn't take very long, and I escaped to my bedroom since I did not want anyone to see me yet. Kelly cleaned up the shaved hair and restored order to the bathroom.

While at the hospital, I had picked up some pamphlets about cancer and lymphoma to use for research. One brochure explained a program run by the Cancer Society called Look Good, Feel Better. The title is self-explanatory. I called to see if I could get an appointment while Kelly was there to go with me. These were supposed to be small classes of eight or fewer which teach ladies how to use makeup to help them feel prettier during chemo treatments. The classes were all full, but the cosmetologist was kind enough to give me an individual class on a Sunday afternoon. Kelly drove me to Utica, New York, and we met the lady behind a BOCES (Board of Cooperative Education Services) building. It seemed clandestine as we waited for her to arrive, since we were the only ones in the parking lot.

Soon she arrived, and we went into a small classroom. I have never worn a lot of makeup over the years, but she encouraged me to use some to give my skin some color. During cancer treatments, most patients don't get a lot of sun and therefore look pale. She especially emphasized how to draw in eyebrows if that hair came out. Thankfully, I did not have to deal with the loss of my eyebrows. They became thinner, and I did lose my eyelashes.

She also gave me a wig and a beautiful scarf with instructions on how to wear them. When we got ready to leave, she gave me two knit caps. One was yellow, and the other was light blue. The knit caps became my close companions; I wore one every night to keep my head warm. I had never known how much warmth my hair had provided. I still had a short stubble of hair, and the caps worked perfectly to keep the short hairs from falling all over the bed. I would wash the hair out of one as I wore the other. The caps were made by volunteers. I was also given a bag containing a myriad of makeup samples. This is an excellent program. I am sure if I had been able to get into a class and was not sick, it would have been fun. I did use some of the makeup to add a little color to my pale skin.

I wore the wig home, and Wayne and John both said it looked good, but it was not me. For one thing, my hair had only started to get a salt and pepper color, and this wig was gray. Also, the style was not even similar to mine. During one of my visits, the doctor told me that most insurances would pay one hundred dollars toward the price of a wig.

Our emotions exploded, and the laughter finally came the next day when Kelly and I decided to go wig hunting. There were two shops near Utica about an hour drive from our home. The first was named after a Statler Brother's song titled "Elvira." With the song going through my mind, I entered the shop and knew at once we had entered *The Twilight Zone*. The salesperson was nice and tried to show me wigs that fit my description, but

I could not find anything that suited me. We left and drove another mile down the street and located the other wig shop. This one was closed. Kelly suggested we get out and look in the window, and there it was—a waist-length, platinum blonde wig with tight curls. As soon as we saw the wig, we both started to laugh as we envisioned me, a fifty-eight-year-old conservative woman, strutting around town and church in that wig, wearing a tight dress and six-inch heels. We laughed all the way home. Kelly and her family left the next day to return to their home in Pennsylvania.

I still did not have a wig! Later that week, I asked my friend Judy Blaas to go with me to look for one. I was able to drive this time, since I knew where we were going and was having a good day. We ended up at a different wig shop, and with her help, I was able to find a suitable one. It was about one hundred fifty dollars. So I paid for it, sent the receipt to the insurance company, and was reimbursed one hundred dollars. It was getting very hot by then, and I found the wig hot, slippery, and itchy. I found out later that there was a cloth that was worn underneath to help with this problem. I think I wore the wig once to church and once out to dinner, and the rest of the time it sat on its stand on the dresser.

I ordered a scarf that tied in the back, and I wore that most of the time. Kelly sewed several more scarfs for me, and I wore them until my hair grew back. I ordered several cute hats, but they did not look good on me. Many people settle for a baseball cap, but I did not like all that bare skin around my neck and ears. Finally, I started to wear scarfs and hats with wide brims. This became my comfortable look. While in the windy city of Buffalo, Wayne would have to chase my hats across the street, dodging cars. Of course, this was dangerous and reminded me of a time when I was a little girl and an elderly man crawled under cars to rescue my Easter hat. Finally, Wayne found a cowboy hat that had an elastic ring around it to hold it snug. This solved the wind problem and looked nice atop my scarfs.

I never knew how vulnerable I would feel without my hair until one morning the mail man brought a package up onto our porch. I was asleep, and I jumped up out of my seat and ran out the door to get the package. I never even thought that I was bald until I saw the image of my bald head in the living room window. I felt so embarrassed, and I'm sure I turned as red as a ladybug. I chatted briefly with the mail man who didn't seem to notice my discomfort. I don't know why I felt so uncomfortable. It was as if I had gone out without my shirt.

One funny incident happened later in the summer when our son's family came to visit. His children were four and two. I had decided I would bring them up to my bedroom to tell them about my baldness. I wanted to let them see me bald instead of them accidently seeing me bald. When I showed them my baldness, they were not upset because their mother had explained to them about my hair. I don't remember Anya saying anything. Sam, the two-year-old, with a big grin, said, "I am afraid you will scare the cat." I laughed, hugged him, and told him he might scare the cat. Then everything was okay. I should not have worried about them seeing me bald. The retelling of this over the years has given us some good laughs. Now I know why the Bible speaks of the woman's hair as being her covering. It really does make me feel protected.

One week in late summer, Kelly, John, and baby Sophia were visiting, and they traveled with us to Cooperstown.

Wayne and John strolled Sophia down to the lake and back. Kelly sat with me while I had the infusion. It was wonderful to have them with us to break up the monotony of the trip. On the way home, we stopped at a café to have lunch. They also sold ice cream cones. We all got one and watched Sophia play outside. Ice cream cones have always been one of my favorite treats, and having a grandchild visit makes even the worst days brighter. As usual, when I got home, I was exhausted and had to lie down.

Later, before another round of treatment, I was surgically fitted with a port, which would make it easier for the oncology nurses to draw blood and to administer the chemo drugs. With the port inserted, I did not have to go to phlebotomy any longer or be pricked with a needle before the nurse administered the chemo drugs. During this time, I had a couple of PET scans. The first one taken after three infusions showed that I was in remission for a brief time. My type of cancer could change its DNA, becoming resistant to the chemo and allowing it to grow again. After the six infusions of CHOP, I was not in remission, and the cancer was growing.

When I awoke from the infusions, I felt fine except for being a bit groggy. Sometimes, Wayne would have to hold me to get me to the car. Sometimes, we would eat at the hospital cafeteria, and sometimes we would stop on the way home to eat. By the time we got home, I was usually tired and would lie down.

I was given a prescription for Allopurinol to take before I started the infusion. It made me break out in a terrible rash with an awful itch. When I saw the doctor the next visit, this medication was removed from my drug list, but the itching and rash lasted for a while. Once or twice a day, I would lie in a bath with a mixture similar to cornmeal that helped with the itching. The bathtub was a disaster to clean. Each infusion after that was mostly uneventful, but it was not unusual to see the doctor turn patients on their head with their feet in the air while still in the chair and leave them for a while. I was blessed to not have many side effects from the chemo drugs. I threw up only once, and it was after eating a lot of fresh pineapple.

After I had finished six rounds of CHOP, I had not gone into remission and was getting sicker. I then had a protocol of two types of chemo ending in the letters *b-e-a-n*. I called these drugs the "bean brothers." These drugs also did not bring me into remission after two six-week rounds.

Next, I had to be admitted to Imogene Bassett hospital for a chemo called ICE. After the infusion, I was required to stay in the hospital with an IV of saline solution for three days to flush the ICE chemo from my system; otherwise, damage to my internal organs would result. They placed me in a room with an elderly woman who was dying. Two members of her family were there languishing by her bed with complete hopelessness, accompanied by moaning, crying, and praying. This situation left me feeling unnerved, and I was on the edge of exploding from anxiety. I was supposed to be put into an isolation room where people had to wear a mask to enter the room. I am a compliant person and will do most things within reason. Having cancer taught me that I had to be my own advocate for my own safety. Thank God I had Wayne for an advocate when he was there, but he could not be there 24/7. Knowing I could not stay there any longer, I grabbed my small bag and a pillow and walked down the hall to a waiting room. I remembered seeing it when we passed by on the way to my room earlier. No one was there, so I laid my pillow down and sprawled on the couch. I did think about germs but figured this was the better of the two choices.

Wayne had gone to park the car and bring in our other belongings, so he did not know where I was. Finally, the nurse found me, and I told her I would not stay in the room with the elderly lady who seemed to be dying. I did not feel this was fair, to her or to me. She explained that they did not have a room on the oncology floor and that it might take a while to get one. I told her I was fine in the waiting room; all I needed was a place to rest. She agreed to let me stay there until she could find another room.

When Wayne arrived, he was able, after some discussion, to get the nurses to understand that I was severely immuno-suppressed and needed to be isolated. I was eventually placed in an isolation room. The day after I had the ICE infusion, an intern stopped by, and for some unknown reason, decided to stop the saline flush. It was 4:45 in the afternoon, and all the oncology doctors were leaving for the day. The oncology desk was not answering the phone. Wayne ran from the hospital across the parking lot to the oncology center and met the supervising oncologist as she was leaving the building. She phoned the hospital and had them restart the saline flush. Those were stressful days!

Wayne and I learned to fight for my health, and this fight occurred on many occasions. I remember a nurse telling us one time that you have to be your own advocate in the hospital, and we learned this was true. There were many times when I was too sick to speak up for myself and was not even aware of all that was happening around me. If Wayne had not been there and willing to go toe-to-toe with the doctors and other medical personnel, plus the people in the business offices, I am not sure what would have happened to me.

A few weeks later, I was at home working in the kitchen while Wayne had gone to work. The phone rang, and I picked it up to speak, but my voice would only squeak. The person on the phone was from the business office at Imogene Bassett Hospital, and I told her that I could not talk. She said to just listen: we would be getting an unusually large bill because our insurance company was not paying for my PET scans. By then, I'd had several of them. I squeaked an *okay* and hung up the phone.

I was wearing a short sleeve shirt that day because it was hot. I looked at my arm and saw a small bump. As I watched, the hives appeared like popcorn popping all down my arm to my wrist. I was trying to think about how to get help because my voice was completely gone. I decided I could call Wayne (this was before smart phones and texting) and just make a noise, and he would know something was wrong. Just as I reached for the phone, Wayne walked in, and he could tell by my actions that something was wrong. He immediately picked up the phone and called the emergency nurse hotline at the oncology department at Imogene Bassett Hospital. He was advised to give me Benadryl if we had any available. If not, to take me to the emergency room. Call an ambulance if I had problems breathing. We were overjoyed to find a box of Benadryl in the medicine chest. After taking a dose of Benadryl, the hives went away as fast as they had arrived. We never did find out what caused this episode. I was extremely grateful that my breathing never was affected. There were a few other times when we needed to call the emergency hotline and were glad to have the phone number taped near the phone.

Even though the PET scans were listed as one of the items covered by my insurance company, they were refusing to pay for them. The hospital was threatening to turn these bills over to a collection agency. I called the insurance company several times to try to see why they were not paying for the PET scans. We were finally able to talk to a person in the Bassett billing office, who agreed to put the bills on hold while we worked with the insurance company. The insurance company kept saying they needed more information before they could approve the payment for these bills but would not give me specific guidelines about what information they needed or how far back the records should go. One day, I became annoyed and asked the person if they needed records from when I was two years old, or if starting after college graduation would be enough. I never could get an answer to this question. Finally, Wayne and I called the records office at Bassett, but they could not send out the records. The next day we drove over to Cooperstown and went to the records office in person. We were allowed to copy my records starting with my first visit with the hematologist-oncologist. While there, we made two copies, one to keep and one to mail to the insurance company. This still did not resolve the issue of the PET scan debts, and it was not resolved until later.

Later in October, my fever spiked, so we went to the emergency room in Hamilton, New York. My bloodwork showed I was neutropenic since my white blood counts were very low—in the danger level. Wayne drove me to Bassett in Cooperstown. I stayed there for ten days in a special room that was supposed to keep out germs. Numerous doctors checked on me, including an infectious disease specialist. Bassett is a teaching hospital, so interns and student doctors came around with the hospitalist several times a day. For several days, I had to lie on a cold pad under my sheet. The purpose was to keep my temperature down. The pad had a small motor which kept ice water circulating around the blanket. It would be the opposite of an electric heating blanket. It didn't work to keep my temperature down. The pad also made my body ache. Finally, I told the hospitalist and a doctor that I refused to lie on that cold pad another day. I suggested they remove the pad from under me and put bags of ice on top of me instead. They agreed to my request, and for the rest of the hospital stay I had ice covering much of my body. This did not keep my temperature down. However, it did not cause me to be in pain like the cooling pad had. During this time, Wayne had to work and could come over only at night. We were over fifty miles from home, and I only had one visitor stop in to see me, a friend from Bible study.

Both Ben and Kelly had driven long hours to see me that day also. Ben left early to go spend some time with his dad and to give Kelly his parking space. They met in the parking lot so that she would not have to drive around looking for a place. Bassett, like many other hospitals, did not have enough parking spaces. We wanted her to have a well-lighted space near the hospital, since she would be leaving after dark. Kelly stayed later into the evening. I did not want her to be driving home late at night, so I told her to leave in time to drive to our home before it became late. Even though she was a mother with a child of her own, she was still my daughter, and I did not want her to drive those dark, curvy roads alone late at night.

One day, while Wayne was there and I was in bed rest-ing, a tall, arrogant, fifty-something man, an oncology doctor, presented himself in the room and talked to Wayne about my diagnosis. An argument ensued. Soon, the man left, and Wayne took off after him in haste. I did not know what was happening but later found out that the doctor was insistent that all of my treatments should be stopped immediately. He believed all of my fevers and swelling were caused by a reaction to the chemo I had already taken, and not cancer. He was not my attending doctor, and I didn't know where my attending doctor was. Many of the oncologists at this cancer center had to work at satellite facilities one or two days a week. This time, Wayne was able to get in touch with my attending doctor, and she sorted out the confusion and rescheduled my PET scan, which the first doctor had canceled for the next week. I do not want to leave the impression that all of my doctors and nurses were hard to deal with, because that is not true. My attending oncologist was a wonderful, caring doctor, who was very knowledgeable about her field and helped me get to Roswell Park Cancer Institute so that I could have a stem cell transplant. According to my experience, there were always a few rotten apples in a bushel. The latest chemo regimen did not bring me into remission, so I had to repeat the "bean" chemo protocol again.

At the end of the ten-day stay, the hospitalist and an associate doctor came into my room late in the afternoon and told me that the fever was caused by the cancer tumors and that there was nothing more they could do. They were releasing me to go home with a fever of 104 degrees. I told the doctors that Wayne would not be able to get me until after he got off from work. I asked the hospitalist if he could talk to Wayne when he got there. He explained that he had been working for twenty-four hours and that he needed to go home. I asked him if he would call Wayne at work and explain the situation, and he agreed.

Wayne had been taking his phone into his classes with him, explaining to the students that if he received a phone call, he would have to take it because I was in the hospital. This was the only class that he had forgotten to take the phone with him, so he missed the doctor's call. As soon as he dismissed class, he saw the phone number from the doctor's call and called him back. The doctor was ugly to him and asked him where he got the number. Wayne reminded the doctor that he had called him first. After that, Wayne was able to get some clarity on the situation.

Wayne drove me home that night in the same exact condition I was in when he drove me to the hospital ten days before. My white counts were up some, but the fever never left. We were on our own, but God was still with us, and we came up with our own solutions for the high fevers, night sweats, and freezing chills.

In early November when the biopsy tissue came back from the lab, my oncologist reemphasized that I had a very aggressive and recurrent type of lymphoma named non-Hodgkin's peripheral angioimmunoblastic T-cell lymphoma. This is a rare type of lymphoma, and she said I would need to have a stem cell transplant soon. She had talked to doctors at Roswell Park in Buffalo and at Dana Farber Cancer Institute in Boston. She asked me which one I would prefer. I asked her which had better results for this type of transplant, and she said they were both excellent. I told her I would go to the one that would take me first.

Wayne had planned to take the family to Hilton Head Island, South Carolina, to celebrate my finishing chemotherapy. By now we knew that I would not go into remission and that I would need the transplant soon. The trip was canceled before we left the hospital to go home. We were later able to get a trip in over Christmas between my routine infusions of the "bean" drugs.

My oncologist called Roswell Park Cancer Institute to tell them that I would be coming there for a transplant. I received a phone call from a secretary from the BMT & Cellular Therapy Team the next day around noon and was asked if I could be there at 1:00 the following afternoon. Of course, I told her, "Yes." I felt excited and hopeful that this was the answer we had been waiting for to find healing for my disease. I had no idea what I would be facing over the next twelve years.

PART II

November 2007: Roswell Park Cancer Institute

Roswell Park Cancer Institute is located in Buffalo, New York, approximately two hundred miles from our home. We had studied the map and knew how to get there by traveling I-90 across central New York. However, the downtown map around the hospital was difficult to read. Later, we found out, one street had two names and only one of them showed up on the map. We got off I-90 and traveled Route 33 west into downtown Buffalo. Even though there was heavy traffic, we were able to find the hospital entrance and use their valet parking. The valet parking was a blessing, since I was too sick to walk very far, and Wayne was not willing to leave me alone while he parked in the parking garage across the street.

We entered this lovely, oval-shaped building with a large waiting area. It had an open ceiling that reached several floors high, and I could see balconies with glass sides on each floor. They opened to the main floor. There was a Steinway grand piano in the large open space, and a pianist played soothing music. Near the center was a coffee shop with pastries. This area remained busy throughout the day. Later, we learned that in the early mornings there would be a line stretching nearly to the door—doctors, nurses, and patients waiting for their morning cup of coffee. From the center of this area to the other outside wall was a large space filled with couches and chairs occupied by people waiting to be seen. Most were patients and their caregivers, dressed in all kinds of garments. This was the middle of a large city, where people from many countries and backgrounds lived. Some had flown to Buffalo, from as far away as Turkey to seek cures for cancer. After soaking up all of this color and sound, we saw a sign that said *registration*. We got into the long line and waited. There were several stations, so the line moved quickly. After giving all of my information, I received my plastic green card and was told not to lose it. It was the ticket to get all the tests needed in this institution. (I still have it but don't plan to use it again.) We were also given instructions to find the BMT (Bone Marrow Transplant) Clinic on the third floor. Wayne got in line for coffee while I sat and rested for a few minutes. Soon we were in line for the elevator. Getting off at the third floor, we found the correct department and checked in at a registration desk before finding a place to wait. The waiting area was nice, and we could hear the music from the grand piano on the first floor. As with any doctor's office or hospital, waiting became a huge part of our experience.

Later, we were taken into an exam room. The first step in any medical office is the taking of vitals. I met several nurses, nurse practitioners, and people from different research groups. They all asked questions and handed me different binders and materials. Many of these overlapped. It seemed that we had waited a long time when the head of the department, Dr. McCarthy, finally entered the room. He immediately told the nurse practitioner to take back the material they had given me about autologous transplants (in these transplants, the patient uses their own stem cells for the transplant). He said that I was too sick for that type of transplant. He made me nervous because I thought I was there to receive that type of transplant. He explained that with my type of cancer and how sick I had been for so long, he thought an allogeneic transplant (a transplant using stem cells from a donor) would be better. He gave me the materials.

The financial director and various nurses met and discussed with us the cost per donor and the number of donors we might need to test. They also explained that the insurance would not cover the cost of testing. Wayne and I peeked at each other with the same thought on our minds: there went the house, the car, and everything else we owned with any monetary value. We knew this transplant was a matter of life and death, and we would use every penny we had. Death was not an option. Each donor had to have six tests initially, and they needed to match me 100 percent on all six tests.

As we discussed donors, I told the doctor that I had two adult children and three brothers. He explained that the children would not be a match because Wayne had "muddied the water." Their DNA was half from me and half from him. My three brothers were tested first since they were the closest to me in DNA. Although they each only had a 25 percent chance of being a match, they were my best chance.

They wanted to test my youngest brother, Mike, first because the younger you are, the more rapidly your body produces T-cells. The doctor saw Wayne and I exchanged looks and asked if there was a problem. I figured he thought we did not get along or there was some other type of problem. I explained to the doctor that Mike's daughter, Michelle, was fighting a cancer battle. She was very sick, and he might not be able to come to Buffalo for the ten days required to harvest the necessary stem cells needed for a transplant. The reason the donor needed to stay in Buffalo for ten days was that the stem cells could not be harvested in one day. If the donor was a match, they had to be evaluated to see if they were healthy enough to be a donor. During the ten-day stay, the donor received daily shots to raise T-cell production. Mike lived in North Carolina, and it would be inconvenient for him to travel this far while his daughter was sick. He agreed to be tested but asked that he could have the blood drawn at Duke in North Carolina instead of traveling to Buffalo. He also wanted to be tested last.

The doctor said his main concern for me was that I would not go into remission long enough for me to have the needed transplant. Usually, a patient has to be in remission in order to go through a transplant. The plan was for me to continue having chemotherapy at Bassett in Cooperstown and come back to Roswell once a month for a checkup. The doctors were hoping I would go into remission so that I could have the transplant in early January.

My middle brother, Larry, who was living in South Carolina, had just started a new job. He was concerned about getting ten days off since he had just been hired. He promised if he was the match, he would come. My older brother, Archie, agreed to be tested, but he'd had heart problems from a young age and was also diabetic. He assumed he might not qualify.

It would cost $3,000 for each person tested, and we might have to test more than ten people. We could easily be looking at over $30,000 just for the testing. Insurance would only cover testing for the donor that was accepted for the transplant. Later, we learned that the five tests had been changed and that each donor kept taking the test only until one was not a match. Each negative match would cost only $600. This still seemed like a lot.

My younger two brothers matched only 20 percent. My older brother matched 40 percent. After some research on my own, I found out that the Leukemia & Lymphoma Society (LLS) offered some financial help to their patients. Also, Roswell Park Cancer Institute had a program that helped patients meet the tremendous cost of cancer treatment. Thankfully, I had to pay out of pocket for my oldest brother's testing only. To help further reduce costs, the initial test could use blood drawn locally and mailed to Roswell Park's phlebotomy laboratory in Roswell's packaging.

I was also able to apply for financial help through the LLS for various local and national programs. The application process was long and arduous, and the rules changed several times over the four years I applied. This money came from donations, and I was, and still am, very thankful for the volunteer donations of funds. As I became healthier, I became a giver of funds for this program instead of a receiver.

Other financial problems included my insurance not paying for my PET scans at Imogene Bassett Hospital in Cooperstown. I had a PET scan every three months along with a CT scan. The insurance paid for the CT scans, but not the PET scans. One day while Wayne and I were both in my room at Bassett, a lady walked in and announced herself a patient advocate. She asked us if we had any concerns about my care while I was in the hospital. At first, I said I could not think of anything. As we visited, it dawned on me that I should ask her about the unpaid PET scans. At this point, they totaled over $30,000 and counting. We explained the situation, and to our surprise, she told us that she would be sitting beside the president of my insurance company for dinner that night and would bring up our situation with him. The next day, I received a phone call from my insurance company agent saying the PET scan debt had been paid.

Later in the next year, we received letters from Roswell Park Cancer Institute saying that we owed $30,000 or more. This was, of course, a shock. Wayne, who was concerned about expenses during this time, was very worried. As we continued to read the letters, they explained we were only getting the letter so we would be aware in case we got a phone call from the New York State Attorney General's office. A bill of $60,000 was sent to the Attorney General's office because the insurance was not covering my bills that they were legally obligated to pay. We never got an actual bill for any of this, and the bills were paid in full. There were other times when we received help with our bills in miraculous ways. God was not only faithful medically, emotionally, and spiritually, but He was faithful with our finances as well.

Because my brothers were not close enough in DNA to be donors, I was placed on the National Donor Registry through the "Be the Match" program. This registry had a large group of donors, over 500,000 from all over the United States. Only four people from that registry matched my DNA.

During our first meeting, Dr. McCarthy explained to me the process for the transplant, and he asked if I understood. I replied, "Sort of." He said we would not leave the room until I understood, and he went through the whole explanation again. I appreciated that he wanted to be sure I understood, but, by this time, I was completely overwhelmed and just wanted to go home. I had a general understanding, so the next time he asked if I understood, I assured him I did. I appreciated his tenacity and am quite sure that there were several times that this quality saved my life.

My chemo schedule was arranged two weeks on and one week off for rest. The oncologist in Cooperstown agreed it would be good for us to go ahead with our family vacation. We had planned to go to Hilton Head Island, South Carolina, with our family earlier that year but had had to cancel. Wayne wanted to give me this trip as a gift for finishing chemotherapy. We rescheduled for Christmas week. We decided to buy presents for the grandchildren only and spend the rest of our money on a house rental. We chose a house with room for our whole family to enjoy Christmas together. I am sure some thought it might be our last Christmas with the family intact.

It was a beautiful house with lots of room, allowing us to enjoy our Christmas together. I felt good, except I tired easily and was emotional, but I was able to enjoy myself. One night, I was cutting up vegetables and nicked a finger. The cut upset me because I had to be so careful about infections. I went to our bedroom to calm myself down. Soon, Kelly came to talk with me, and I explained that the very small things in my life had somehow become huge for me. After we visited for a while, I was able to go back to the dining room and enjoy dinner. Most of the week was pretty uneventful. Before we left for this vacation, I had managed to bake some sugar cookies to bring along for us to decorate. This was one of our family traditions. My sweet, friend Delores knew that this was one of our family traditions, and sensing that I was worried about baking enough desserts, arrived the day before we left with a gift of sugar cookies.

It was important to me to try to make things as normal as possible during this week. We put Christmas lights around an orange tree and placed the grandchildren's presents underneath. They were happy to see the gifts. The type of tree didn't matter. I cut paper strips to make paper chains, and Kelly brought lights to decorate the tree. It was beautiful. We had a wonderful vacation with the family together.

At the end of the week, we came home and continued my schedule of chemo. Now we were going to Buffalo once a month, and my brothers had started their tests to see if they would be a match. The psychologist at Roswell was concerned about the patients having something to keep their minds occupied during the long hospital stay. My chiropractor at Hamilton had told me about a friend of hers who'd had a similar transplant. She had used a blog to help keep her family and friends informed of her progress. I thought the blog was a good idea. When the psychiatrist at Roswell Park asked how I planned to keep my mind occupied, I told her about the blog. She told me that Roswell Park had just started their own blog called "Care Pages." She explained the advantages of being able to give everyone the same information at the same time. Blogging was one way of keeping confusion and rumors down.

The blog was also helpful when I had been sick and in the

hospital. Wayne would get annoyed if he had a lot of phone calls to make after he came home from spending hours at the hospital. The blog also gave family and friends the ability to send messages of care and hope. It became a real lifeline for us. We called only our moms and children; everyone else got their information from the blog. That blog housed good anecdotal information that I eventually used in this book. It shone light on authentic feelings and actions that were taking place on the spot. We updated the blog almost daily and sometimes more. Wayne wrote much of it in the beginning since I was too sick to concentrate. I have always loved to read, but to my surprise, after the transplant, I was not able to focus for a few weeks. Sometimes I could read just one or two pages at a time.

PART III

March 2008: Welcome to Evelyn's Blog and Reflections

Wayne made my handle "Biker Teacher" because we had been taking motorcycle trips since 2006, and I was a teacher. He did not ask me about this handle, and I was sure some people wondered why he chose the name. Following each entry in the blog, I have added my thoughts concerning the entry and the day's events in "Evelyn's Reflections."

March 1, 2008, 6:17 p.m. – Wayne

Welcome to Evelyn's Blog!

I will try to keep you posted each day as we travel through this latest adventure. Please keep in mind that I can't spell and that there is no spell check on this program.

Yesterday we received good news. We are full steam ahead

for the transplant. The schedule is as follows:

Tuesday, March 4, 2008, Evelyn goes to Cooperstown for what will hopefully be her last day of chemo there. It will be a single day of chemo.

March 5–6, she will be in Buffalo for a series of pretransplant tests. On March 5, her donor will have her physical.

March 11 or 12, Evelyn will be admitted to Roswell Transplant Unit (BMT) and will start a series of chemo cocktails lasting six days and wiping out her existing immune system.

On March 17 and 18, the stem cells will be harvested from her donor.

On March 19, Evelyn will be infused with the new stem cells.

All of the above is tentative, and we are waiting for a fax with the exact schedule.

The point is that we are getting close.

For the past two weeks, Evelyn has been having fevers of 102 to 106 degrees, chills, and extreme joint pain. Her feet and hands are swollen, making it difficult for her to walk, write, or open a bottle of water. Usually, the fevers start around 2:00 p.m. and last until 8 or 9 a.m. She also has severe soaking night sweats. Today, we started a regimented series of Tylenol every four hours even when she feels well. So far this afternoon (7 p.m.), she has no fever but a little chill.

Evelyn's Reflections:

I had a fever every day for over a year. When we were camping and it became hot, I would take my lawn chair and sit it into a cool, Adirondack lake. This began a ritual of Wayne getting a pan of ice water where I could soak my feet to bring down the fever. Knowing that a chill would follow, Wayne would put his heavy fleece robe into the dryer to heat it up. If he put the hot robe over me with one or two blankets on top, I would warm up quickly.

Some nights, I would change pajamas three to five times because I would wake up drenched every few hours. We were both too tired to change the sheets, so I would pile dry towels over the wet spot until the next day. I would be frozen by the time I got back into bed, and Wayne would hug me as tightly as he could and snuggle the blankets around me like a swaddled baby. The next night we would repeat the process. Wayne would wash the pajamas and towels each day. Finally, we had to leave the heat up at night so that I was not as chilled after I changed my pajamas.

March 2, 2008, 4:58 p.m. – Wayne

Evelyn officially retired on March 1, 2008. That was a hard decision to make, as she really wanted to get twenty years teaching in New York State and was so close. We spent a week filing papers with the New York State Teachers' Retirement System and Social Security. Today, it became obvious that the latest chemo (ICE) is making her hair disappear again. That was discouraging, even though we knew the hair would come out. If the (ICE) treatment didn't cause it to come out, the strong chemo at Roswell to get her ready for the transplant would. For Evelyn, that is very discouraging.

She has been very tired today. The fevers came back last night, only lower (102.5 max) and lasted until noon today. She also had a few hives, but not bad. The doctors cannot tell us what is causing the fevers and the sweats. They all have a different opinion, and some say they just don't know. Tomorrow we hope to have a fax from Roswell telling us the schedule for transplant. We will share it when we have it.

Evelyn's Reflections:

While we were at Hilton Head Island for Christmas, my hair had grown about three fourths of an inch and made me feel a bit more normal. I didn't feel I had to hide behind a scarf all the time. Having it come out again made me feel like I was going backward.

In the fall of 2007, Wayne was still working and trying to take care of me at the same time. I knew Jesus was my ultimate advocate, but as a little boy once prayed, "sometimes you need someone with skin on." As I was given a round of chemo, I had a ton of fluids infused at the same time to flush the chemo and the dead cancer cells out of my body. My lungs started to fill with fluid, and I could not breathe. Pulmonary doctors were called, and I was given a large dose of Lasix to help the fluids pass. As my breathing resumed normalcy, all I wanted was to go home.

Originally, the doctors told me I could probably go home on the afternoon of the third day. Finally, one of the doctors told me if I could pee another gallon of urine, I could go home. Now I had a goal. It had always been a family joke about how much and how often the members of the Collie family went to the bathroom. Well, I was a Collie before I married Wayne, so this was a chore I could relate to. Before long, I was able to go home.

March 3, 2008, 8:20 p.m. — Wayne

Well, it feels like Evelyn is on her way to a transplant. We got the official schedule today for this week.

Tuesday, March 4, be in Cooperstown at 9:30 a.m., meet with the doctor, and hopefully get the last chemo at Cooperstown.

Wednesday, March 5, be in Buffalo at 9:30 a.m. for a meeting with the transplant team (family meeting) and caretakers. Then pretransplant testing the rest of the day. Should be done by 4 p.m. We will stay in Buffalo that evening.

Thursday, March 6, more pretransplant testing and then return home that night.

Cooperstown is about an hour and forty-five minutes each way, and Buffalo is three hours and forty-five minutes each way. The weather forecast predicts rain, freezing rain, and finally eight inches of snow tomorrow and tomorrow night. We will leave early.

Evelyn had a good night and day. Her fever did not go over 100.5.

Her hair is becoming a problem, and we will most likely shave it all off again tomorrow night.

Evelyn Reflections:

Since we did not have any family members nearby or anyone available to stay, my wonderful friend, Miriam Cross, came with us to the family meeting. One of the purposes of the meeting was to have someone other than the main caregiver understanding the seriousness and guidelines to which I would have to adhere for the transplant. There were several times when Miriam stayed with me while Wayne had to be elsewhere. She became the sister I never had biologically. We had a lot in common since we were both from southern roots and married northern men. God provided Miriam to both Wayne and me during this time, and she was a wonderful blessing to us and still is today.

March 4, 2008, 6:39 p.m. – Wayne

Evelyn had her last chemo today at Cooperstown. Everything went fine. The reason she has been so tired this past week is that she is anemic. The doctor said they may give her a transfusion tomorrow at Roswell Park. The swelling in her feet and hands is a symptom or result of her disease. Most of her hair fell out today, so I gave her a buzz cut tonight. That made it look more even and would not drive her crazy. We are off to Buffalo tomorrow morning. We will leave about 5:00 a.m., hoping the freezing rain will be turned to rain by then. No fevers today.

Evelyn's Reflections:

In all our trips to Buffalo or Cooperstown, we never had a lot of problems with snow. Buffalo is well known for its huge amounts of snowfall. Often, the sky dumps several inches in just an hour. Again, God protected us. We did drive through some snow, but we were always just a little ahead or a little behind the worst of the storm. I know this was God's protection because he always made a way for me, just as he did the Israelites in the desert.

Interstate 90 crosses New York from Albany to Buffalo along Lake Ontario, Lake Erie, and the Finger Lakes. It is often closed down because of lake-effect snow. In over eight years of travel, often several times a week, it was never closed when we needed to go.

Once, we had a huge snowfall in Eaton, and a large tree fell across our driveway blocking our path to the road. Wayne had to cut the tree and move it out of the driveway before we could begin our trek. Just before we were ready to leave, our electricity went off. We had a generator but could not leave it running while we were gone. Finally, I called the BMT Clinic and told them I could not come until the next day. When I got there, the doctor told me to not change my appointments. I might have been anemic, but my blood boiled. That was the only appointment we had changed in over eight years, and we had never missed a single appointment. I'd call that a pretty good batting average.

Often, when things were getting a bit tough, a good friend would write a Scripture or a song lyric on my blog post at just the right time. A friend from school, Sue Cross, sent me a verse from "His Eye Is on the Sparrow." God had woken her up and put that song on her mind. She knew it was for me. She prayed for me in the middle of the night, and the next morning sent me these words:

Let not your heart be troubled, His tender word I hear.
And resting on his goodness, I lose my doubts and fears.
Tho' by the path He leadeth, but one step I may see:
His eye is on the sparrow, and I know He watches me:
His eye is on the sparrow and I know He watches me.

March 5, 2008, 2:24 p.m. – Wayne

Well, we are back from Roswell Park. It was a very disappointing trip. Yesterday went well. We had the family meeting, signed all the advanced directives, talked about some trials with the doctor, and Evelyn completed all the tests that were scheduled for her. She was supposed to have a few remaining tests today, return home, and then be admitted for the transplant next week on March 13. About 5:00 p.m., after we had returned to the motel, the Transplant Coordinator called and told us the donor did not show for her physical. We will have to find another donor! This is the second time this has happened. They do have a different donor that is a close match, but she needs to be a 100 percent match. They also need to find out if she is willing to donate and if she can pass the physical. This could take an additional month or longer. Once we find out all of this, Evelyn will need to take the pretransplant test again, and then we will proceed from there.

The doctors are worried about the extra time since the cancer has flared up or returned several times. They are also afraid of her cancer coming back again, stronger, in a different location or form. To say the least, we are disappointed. However, we have done everything we can and are not in control of what happens. This is a particularly hard day for Evelyn. She is coming down from the steroid and is very tired. We left the house at 4:00 a.m. yesterday. As of now, she is scheduled to continue chemo at Cooperstown starting again on Tuesday of next week. We can only wait to see what happens with the donor. Evelyn appreciates all of your thoughts and prayers and especially reading your messages.

Evelyn's Reflections:
After I was diagnosed and unable to go back to school in the fall, I started going to a Bible study in Hamilton called "Interwoven Hearts." We were studying the book of Isaiah and one of the verses about God being on the throne. At that time, the presence of the Lord surrounded me, and I knew that whatever happened to me would be okay. God was still on his throne and would remain on the throne, no matter how my journey proceeded. That truth kept me strong through many disappointing moments of this journey. I have always been able to find a silver lining in every cloud. I was so thankful that I had

only completed the less complicated and invasive test, so when I had to do them over it was not as awful as it could have been.

During some of my hardest times, people would write encouraging words or quote Bible verses. At this time, my niece, Maria, quoted Philippians 4:4–7 (KJV):

> Rejoice in the Lord always, and again I say, rejoice! Let your moderation be known unto to all men. The Lord is at hand. Be careful for nothing; but in everything by prayer and supplication, with thanksgiving, let your requests be known unto God; and the peace of God, which passeth all understanding, shall keep your hearts and minds through Christ Jesus.

This was the perfect passage for that day.

March 8, 2008, 5:24 p.m. — Wayne

It is a cold, wet, dreary day here. There is no question that Evelyn has come off the steroids that she received with her chemo last Tuesday. The swelling in her feet is much better, but her joints are painful today, she has a fever, she is very tired, and had the first real chill since Tuesday. I placed a heavy robe in the dryer to heat it up and then put it on her to get her warm. Tonight, she also needed the heating pad. She rode with me to Walmart this morning but did not get out of the car. Maybe that is why she is so tired. It will be a long thirty days waiting for the new donor. If she could stand to travel, I would take her someplace where it was warm, and the sun was shining. Maybe next fall we can go to Oktoberfest in Daytona. She really does enjoy your messages. Have a great weekend.

Evelyn's Reflections:

Let me describe the effects of the steroids on the body and mind. The "P" in CHOP stands for Prednisone, which is a steroid. The day after the chemo, I would take a large dose of steroids and then wean them down each day until I was off. The steroids made me very hyper and unable to sleep. The first day, while the dosage was high, I would look for things to alphabetize. After five days, I would be off and have a down, sometimes weepy, day. We were a bit naïve and thought that I would be back to normal by fall. Wayne even asked one of the nurses if she thought the doctor would give us permission to take a motorcycle trip out West in late fall. Needless to say, it is a good thing that we did not know the length of time this journey would take.

March 9, 2008, 8:48 p.m. – Wayne

It has been a good day. Last night was really tough with fever, sweats, and chills. She has had none today yet. If you are interested in a good website for learning about different types of cancer, the doctors recommend www.cancer.org. Evelyn's disease is non-Hodgkin's peripheral angioimmunoblastic T-cell lymphoma, or non-Hodgkin's T-cell lymphoma. It is a rare, aggressive type of lymphoma that can change its DNA over time, making it hard for the chemo to stay ahead of the disease.

The protocol at Roswell, when we get there, will involve completely wiping out her immune system. She will not be able to have fruit unless it is cleaned well with a vinegar water solution and no berries or grapes because they are hard to wash. Only artificial flowers are permitted. Visitors have to wear a mask and gloves while in her room. Also, no live plant matter is allowed in her room since mold and fungi are very dangerous to her as she waits for the donor cells to engraft and her immune system to increase.

March 11, 2008, 7:00 p.m. – Evelyn

Hello, all. I had chemo today and am still anemic. I had a shot to bring the red cells up to normal, and tomorrow I will have a shot to bring the white ones up. Thankfully, I get the shot the day after chemo at my primary care doctor's office in Hamilton. That saves me another tiring trip to Cooperstown after every chemo regimen. Other than being tired, I have had a good day.

For some reason, neither Wayne nor I slept very well last night. I had to change into dry pajamas three times, but my temperature stayed down, and I didn't have a chill.

Today was somewhat sunny for central New York, and even though it was cold, Wayne was able to get in a walk both in Hamilton and in Cooperstown. Walking has become a sanity saver for Wayne.

We were blessed with an unexpected gift from a charity today which will help us pay our travel expenses. God is faithful and is meeting our practical needs as well as our physical and spiritual needs.

Since my chemo date has been postponed, I decided to get my eyes checked and will probably need new glasses. I have an eye appointment tomorrow and may have new spectacles to take to Roswell.

Thanks to everyone for your messages of encouragement. They are meaningful, and I enjoy hearing from all of you. Love, Evelyn

March 11, 2008, 11:23 p.m. — Evelyn

Hello all.

Early this evening, Wayne had to go to Walmart, which is about twenty-five miles north of us, to get some supplies. While he was gone, I slept hard on the couch. When I woke up with a jolt, I took my temperature, and it was 106 degrees. This frightened me, so I called my daughter-in-law, Yolanda. Keep in mind that she lives eight hours south of me. I felt too weak to get up for ice water to bath my feet.

Yolanda talked with me and kept me calm until Wayne came home a few minutes later. As soon as he came in, we started our ritual for dealing with fevers and chills.

It is a little late to be blogging, and two in one day is a lot; however, my mind is blogging in the bedroom, so I will see if my fingers will cooperate for a few minutes. I am a little itchy, and the steroids are keeping me awake tonight. I took a Benadryl, which should take care of both problems soon.

Cancer is quite an up and down disease. Some days I still don't believe this is me. Who is that person in the mirror with that Yule Brenner haircut? Other days I know all too well: it is me going through this awful experience. Then when I see others getting chemo and experiencing much worse side effects, I know I am truly blessed. Most of my chemo treatments last only about two and a half hours. The timing depends on how long it takes to get the blood test back and how busy they are in the chemo room. The drugs are so expensive that they are not mixed until the bloodwork shows I am able to take them. That way they are fresh and potent. If I am not able to get them because of my blood counts, they are not wasted.

I am presently getting only two chemotherapy drugs, but there are other pre-drugs that are given mostly for nausea and relaxation. One of them is a steroid that takes about two days to wear off. On the day that drug wears off, I am usually very tired and also down emotionally, leading to a sleepy, crying day. It helps to know that most of this is due to the drugs, and it will pass soon. Instead of being upset with myself on those days, I allow myself to know that I really don't have a lot of control because of the drugs. It is okay. Wayne does not like to see me cry because he can't do anything to fix my problem. I usually go to bed, and after I cry, I go to sleep. Sleeping is the most peaceful thing I can do.

Presently, I am getting chemo two weeks in a row, followed by a rest week. This pattern will continue until I have a donor ready to harvest their T-cells, and then I will be admitted to Roswell for seven days (or a day minus six) prior to harvest date. Before I am admitted, I have to undergo two days of testing to gain data which will be used to compare with data from after the transplant. Infusion day is day zero and my new birthday. I will be in the hospital in semi-isolation for thirty days. After being released from the hospital, we will live in an apartment in Buffalo for at least one hundred days. This is, if everything goes according to plan. We have to be within fifteen minutes of the hospital at all times, and I cannot be left alone. It is a good thing Wayne and I like each other. At first, I will have to go back to the hospital every day to be checked and sometimes receive platelets.

This ended up being much longer than I had anticipated. Good night to all. Love, Evelyn

March 13, 2008, 4:36 p.m. – Evelyn

Hi all. I called the Transplant Coordinator on Wednesday morning and learned that the second donor has agreed to donate. She is scheduled for her physical on Friday, March 21. Pray she is able to keep her appointment, is well, and can donate.

Today I feel pretty well and have kept busy doing some housework. Kelly and her family are coming tonight for a few days, and that gives us something to anticipate. She is expecting her baby on April 19, so this will be her last visit for a while. This is just a short update for today. Since I have been busy, I feel the need for a nap before supper. Take care and love to all.

March 15, 2008, 4:28 p.m. – Wayne

Today is kind of a down day. Evelyn is very tired and was cold and achy most of the day. The weather is cold also. The fevers are gone now (5:00 p.m.), but they always leave her tired. She was up five times because of sweats last night. On the bright side, Kelly, John, and Sophia are here for the weekend. Their visits always brighten up the house. Evelyn wants me to take a picture of her without hair and post it, and I will as soon as I get a chance to take one. Have a good weekend.

Evelyn's Reflections:

I decided when we started the blog that I wanted to be authentic in sharing the good and the bad. I hated the way I looked without hair, but baldness is a big part of the cancer journey, and I decided not to hide it. I was very happy when my hair grew back. It was tight curly at first with reddish ends, but it eventually looked normal with less gray. The one positive among the negatives.

Evelyn and I decided it might be a good idea to post a picture that shows the reality of her situation, especially for those who live far away. The other pictures, taken just a few short months ago, show Evelyn much healthier and bring to mind happy memories. It was a particularly good morning with no fevers, no chills, and minimal pain. It was a happy day because Kelly, John, and our granddaughter were here.

The disease Evelyn has is called non-Hodgkin's T-cell lymphoma. It is a very aggressive, recurrent cancer. When it was discovered last May, it was well advanced and present in all of her lymph nodes, spleen, and liver but no other organs. This is labeled Stage 4. One of the characteristics of this cancer is that it can change its DNA, becoming resistant to chemotherapy. This resistance has happened three times during the last nine months. The chemo being used now is a combination of two chemo drugs that are keeping a lid on the cancer but not eliminating it.

The stem cell/bone marrow transplant we are waiting for is a very serious, dangerous procedure. In order for Evelyn to receive the donor stem cells and thus a new immune system, the doctors will use a series of chemo infusions over a six-day period. They will completely eliminate her immune system. A mold or fungus in the air caused by a farmer plowing a field or someone mowing their grass can be lethal. She will be susceptible to infections for at least a year. Once the transplant is completed, it will take about four weeks for the donor cells to engraft or take hold. Engrafting does not always happen, and the transplant may need to be repeated, unless Evelyn is not too sick by then to even consider it. Once the donor cells engraft, the next risk is graft-versus-host disease, or rejection. This is common, serious, and potentially lethal, occurring in about 30 percent of the cases. Normally, they would like to harvest stem cells from Evelyn's own blood. This will not work for her because her immune system is weak, and her cancer has proven to be particularly aggressive and resistant.

We are moving forward with the transplant because we have no choice. Without the transplant, she will not survive. Even though it is a very risky procedure, it is our only option. The transplant needs to happen very quickly as she is becoming weaker every day. She has trouble walking up and down stairs because of joint pain. She can no longer open a soda bottle because of joint pain and muscle weakness, and she is short of breath and exhausted. Her body feels like she has the flu constantly. Can you imagine having a severe case of the flu for ten long months? For example, the picture was taken at 9:30 a.m., and now it is 2:00 p.m., and the fevers are back (101.8). I will start feeding her ice chips and bathing her feet in ice water to keep it from going extremely high. She will probably have a fever, at some level, until she goes to bed tonight, and then the night sweats start, causing her to change pajamas four or five times.

We need to move forward as soon as possible. The doctors at Roswell and her doctors at Cooperstown are concerned the cancer will flare up stronger and more resistant, or in a different form, rendering the transplant useless. I don't know how to emphasize the seriousness of her situation any stronger, and I have most likely understated it simply because it is hard to admit even when we are living it. I want everyone to know that this is a very serious situation. Because of the disease and treatment requirements, time is of the essence. Finally, I want to emphasize how proud I am of Evelyn as she is dealing with this. She is one *fantastic lady*. We are in need of prayers.

Evelyn's Reflections:
Even now, in 2020, it is hard for me to read this passage. It brings tears to my eyes to remember the condition I was fighting every day. I am so proud of Wayne and his tremendous effort to help me in this battle. Some refer to cancer as "the Beast," and it is an accurate description of the cell-destroying disease. It was only by the grace and mercy of God that we were able to overcome. We fought this battle together with God's help.

March 17, 2008, 1:10 p.m. – Evelyn
Hello. I am back. Some days I am just too tired to get my thoughts together to write a paragraph. Most of you are familiar with my odd expressions, but some days when Wayne asks me how I feel, the only way I can express my feelings is to say that I feel like a wet dishrag. Some days I feel as if I have been run over by a dump truck. Another day, I may feel like a party balloon after the party is over—deflated and left on the ground, to be walked over by the happy dancers. Other days, I feel alone even though I know God is with me. On days when I have a high fever, I feel like a pincushion with shards of ice blowing against my skin. Sometimes people make fun of me for saying these expressions, but they are my feelings and my expressions. I do not have to explain them.

Most days have a high, middle, and low point. Usually, the high point comes first thing in the morning, and when I want to accomplish anything, then I need to get right to work. I have two to three hours maximum to get anything done. That includes a shower and a little housework, and I do mean a little. Next comes a nap and then waiting for Wayne to get home from work. By mid-afternoon, I am usually tired and need a late afternoon nap to get the energy to eat the supper Wayne has prepared. After supper, I need another nap so I can stay up until 10:00 in order to take meds before going to bed for the night. At some time during the day, I usually muster enough strength to fold a load of clothes Wayne has washed. Other than that, I still read and work on simple puzzles. I don't enjoy TV, so I listen to Christian music during the day. One of the highlights of my day is when either Wayne or I check my messages to hear from my friends and family. I usually receive several wonderful, positive, caring notes with prayers, Scriptures, and kind words. It is good to know what is happening outside my sterile world. It is easy to become depressed at a time like this, but I can keep it at bay by listening to my praise music and reading your encouraging words. Today I had a lovely visit with three friends who encouraged me with warm words, prayers, and hugs. A few people have sent me copies of healing verses in the Bible. I read these and believe they apply to me.

This weekend Ben, Yolanda, and their two children will be here from Virginia. Even though the weather doesn't look promising, their visit will bring some sunshine into our lives. Thank you all for reading my messages and keeping in touch. Even the people who don't reply—I know you are there.

March 18, 2008, 11:00 a.m. – Wayne
We just found out this morning that the donor decided not to participate. Now we are searching for a new one. This puts the

earliest date for transplants off for thirty days or longer. It is extremely frustrating that people will sign up and agree to be a donor and then not follow through. As of now, three people have done this, costing us about three months. One decided not to donate when they were first called. The first harvest date was to have been February 10. If we find a suitable donor, it could be the end of April or the first of May now. Needless to say, we are devastated.

Evelyn's Reflections:
I try to give people the benefit of the doubt, and I am sure that when people sign up to donate, they have good intentions, but things happen to interfere. I have to trust that God has a better match for me since this person was not a 100 percent match. We will wait and pray for a better match soon.

March 19, 2008 7:24 p.m. – Wayne
Many of you have asked about the possibility of becoming a donor for Evelyn. It is not a simple process, and I have asked the transplant coordinator at Roswell Park for some clear, concise answers for you. These answers are valid as of 2008.

*The odds of an individual person becoming the match for a particular person are astronomical. For example, siblings have a 25 percent chance of a match. Evelyn's three brothers were not a match.

*There are over five hundred thousand potential donors and thirty thousand cord blood units in the US registry. Even with that number, there may not be a match for a particular individual or at most one or two.

A match is not as simple as a blood type. A match means

that the human leukocyte antigens (proteins on the body's cells that the body uses to recognize which cells belong to you and which do not) in your body match the recipient's. A child's chance of matching a parent are no better than the general population. The doctor explained to me that this is because I have polluted the gene pool.

If you are interested in joining the registry (meaning that you are willing to donate to anyone), you can do so by going online to www.marrow.org/join. They will send you a kit to use to swab your check and send back to them. The fee for the kit is about fifty-five dollars, which covers the cost of the test, and must be paid by the donor.

If you specify that the test is specifically for an individual, then the testing must be done privately. It is very expensive and is not covered by insurance. The costs for testing Evelyn's brothers were several thousand dollars.

We appreciate your desire to help. I am not sure I have all the answers for you, but I hope the above helps. It is absolutely amazing to us that there is a worldwide registry of over five million people. The next donor the center is looking for is international. If you want more information about the National Marrow Donor Program, go to the web address.

March 24, 2008, 2:59 p.m. – Evelyn
Hello everyone. I sweated through several pairs of pjs last night and had a chill and fever early this morning. I don't know how I could sweat so much while lying still. I woke up feeling cold and wet, so I had to change. Once the fever broke this morning, I had a nap around 11:00 a.m., and then I felt better. I was able to wash all the wet PJs and do a little vacuuming. Yolanda did

all of the cooking while she was here, so we have some nice leftovers. Wayne can cook also and does a nice job.

A friend brought us a big pot of soup for the weekend and some chocolate chip cookies. I froze part of the soup and cookies for another day. Another friend brought stuffed shells and cookies. As you can see, we are eating well. People have sent me devotional books, CDs, novels, and puzzle books, along with lotions and other things to brighten my days. Friends from Wayne's office sent me a large basket of unique gifts to help me keep my mind occupied as well as help with skin care. My friend from work, Pat Gunther, brought me a huge basket filled with all types of thoughtful gifts.

As many have recognized, the waiting is hard. As long as I am able to get out some and do a little housework, the days go by quickly. I am really trying to, and most of the time, I'm successful at being thankful each day. Kelly loaned me a book about the true story of a woman who wrote down things she was thankful for every day. Her goal was to reach a thousand things she was thankful for in her daily life. I made a list for a while, but I did not need to reach a thousand in order to understand that joy comes through thanksgiving. I thank God that his mercies are new each day. "Great Is Your Faithfulness" is one of my favorite hymns.

I love spring and am ready to see some green grass and flowers, just as I know you all are. However, in central New York, spring is a long way off in March. Spring, as well as Easter, is a sign of new birth and God's grace for each one of us.

Tomorrow is chemo day. The steroids usually make me hyper for a couple of days. Don't be surprised if you get a midnight blog or a picture of me swinging from the chandelier. Continued thanks go out to all who are reading this blog, and thanks for all your prayers and kind words. I love you all.

March 25, 2008, 12:46 p.m. – Wayne

We came home from Cooperstown early today. The doctor decided to stop the current chemo treatment because the side effects seem to be outweighing the benefits. Evelyn declines a little each day. The doctor wants to restage her with new PET scans to see where the cancer is now and what condition it is in. Then we move onto a more aggressive treatment. Evelyn will have the PET scan on Thursday of this week, and we will get the results next Tuesday. In some ways, this is disappointing because it is a confirmation of what we suspected, but in other ways it is moving on to something different. We do not have any news about a new donor. I called the transplant coordinator several times and just got a recording. Evelyn's time is running out.

March 25, 2008, 5:47 p.m. – Wayne

This disease has its ups and downs. Just when you are ready to choke anything and anyone in your path, things change. We received a call today from Roswell Park with a donor and a schedule to transplant. We leave to go for tests on Wednesday, March 26, and return home the evening of March 27. Then we return to Roswell on Friday, April 4, to have a Hickman (infusion line similar to a port, but with three lines) implanted. Evelyn will then be admitted to the hospital on Sunday, April 6, to start getting ready for six days of chemo. At the end of the six days, on Saturday, April 12, she will be infused with the donor stem cells and have a new immune system. There are still some things that have to happen: the donor has to pass her physical,

Evelyn has to pass the rest of her tests including a PET scan on Thursday, and the stem cells have to be harvested. The donor is international. Tomorrow, I will call Bassett to cancel her PET scan. Hallelujah, we are on our way once more. Maybe the fourth time is the charm. Please pray that everything falls into place this time. She is getting very tired and weak.

March 26, 2008, 6:21 p.m. – Wayne

We are in Buffalo. Evelyn actually feels pretty good tonight—no fevers, just tired. In case anyone is wondering, parking is much easier and cheaper in Morrisville and Eaton. I will let you know tomorrow night how the day goes. The final and most dreaded test (bone marrow biopsy) is scheduled for Friday at 12:30, so we should be able to come home Friday evening. We both feel good about this. God has brought us this far, and I am sure he will continue to lead us, whatever the result. We are in his hands.

March 27, 2008, 4:44 p.m. – Wayne

We were able to finish all the tests today. The results we have so far were all good. We will find out the other results tomorrow. I assume if there is a problem, they will call us. The doctors made clear that Evelyn has had all the chemo she can tolerate. Her body is starting to react. She has been on chemo for over ten months. She is very tired, and it was a long, rough day, but we are done with the tests. We will return for surgery for the placement of the Hickman on Friday, April 4. After that, we will stay here in Buffalo for her to be admitted on Sunday morning. I have an apartment lined up for me, and then for us both after she is out of the hospital. That is all for now. My brain is fried.

March 30, 2008, 12:47 p.m. — Evelyn

Hello. First, I would like to say thank you to the students in Ms. Hammond's class who made me the beautiful lap quilt. You guys are awesome, and I love you all. I would love to give you all a hug. You also have a wonderful teacher to take time to do this for me. The picture Wayne put on the blog is not a nice one of me, but it shows the quilt nicely. My neck is swollen from the steroids, and it makes me look like a linebacker.

One of my biggest concerns right now is that I have lost my voice from a swollen lymph node pressing on my voice box. It is raspy and comes and goes and makes it very difficult to talk on the phone. Wayne and I are quite a pair. He can't hear, and I can't talk above a whisper. We get by though. I am really hoping this swelling goes away soon. I am sure there will be other side effects from the drugs I start on Sunday, but hopefully none of them will be permanent. This is one way to learn patience. I am still not good at being patient. The Lord must feel that I need some remediation.

Wayne and I are thinking about what we need to take with us to Buffalo and what needs to be done here before we go next Thursday. It is hard to do this because we have not seen the apartment and do not know what is there. I know it is furnished and has basic cooking items, but I'm not sure what else. We finally decided that Wayne would have to make more than one trip.

Wayne spent most of the day working on taxes and making sure our finances are in order. He moved money from savings to checking accounts, because we do not know what our expenses will be while we are in Buffalo. I packed and organized the house as much as I could with my limited energy level. Earlier,

Babysitting Anya and Sam

Boating with Kelly

Wayne and Sam, 2005

Leaving airport, Sioux Falls, South Dakota

Riding the Bear Tooth, Montana, 2006

Lake McDonald, Glacier National
Park, Montana

Quilt sewn by Ms. Hammond's class

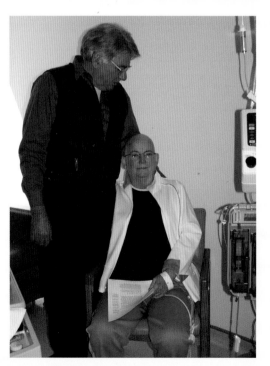

Wayne and I, my hospital room, Roswell Park

Me with my pole, showing some of my medications

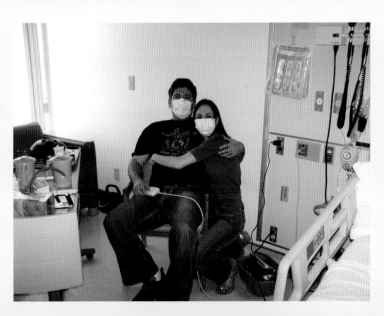

Ben and Yolanda waiting for my transplant,
Roswell Park

Walking
with my pole

Me holding Solomon,
Buffalo apartment

Wayne, Sophia,
and Solomon,
Buffalo apartment

A brief escape to
Niagara Falls

A new adventure, Camp Joy,
Pennsylvania, 2018

Backyard, Virginia, 2020

I had bought some comfortable sweatpants and tops to wear in the hospital. I am too swollen to wear my regular clothes. There is a laundry facility near the BMT where Wayne can keep my laundry clean. I am not allowed to wash clothes even after I get out of the hospital. I can fold them and put them away.

I need to go; I am very tired. Love to all.

April 2, 2008, 10:21 a.m. – Wayne

I called the transplant coordinator at Roswell this morning and she told me the donor passed her physical, had blood drawn, and as far as she knows, everything is a go. She is, however, still waiting for some more information from the donor and wants to call us before we leave for Buffalo tomorrow afternoon. So far, no negative news, but a lot of things need to fall into place for this process to continue. She also confirmed that all of the test Evelyn took last week were good and that the PET scan was a little better than the last one.

April 3, 2008, 11:56 a.m. – Wayne

I talked to the transplant coordinator this morning, and everything is all set. The car is almost packed, the refrigerator is empty, and the garbage is at the dump. If I can get to a computer tomorrow, I will let everyone know how the surgery for the Hickman went. The biggest concern now is that she has to stop taking some of her pain medicine this morning since it thins the blood. As soon as the surgery is completed tomorrow, she can start the pain medicine again. We will keep up the webpage as often as we can. Thanks for the messages and prayers.

Evelyn's Reflections:

I feel like we are getting ready to launch a space rocket with all the details we are juggling daily. We need a secretary and an engineer, but we will settle for prayer.

April 4 2008, 2:19 p.m. — Wayne

The Hickman lines are in, and we are in a room at Kevin Guest house. Evelyn is tired and having a chill. Everything went well, and we are scheduled for admittance and the first chemo on Sunday morning. The doctor wants to see her tomorrow morning as he is concerned about her chills and fevers. They drew cultures this morning just to make sure she does not have an infection. Every doctor she sees takes cultures because they can't believe she has as many fevers as she does. The cultures always come out negative. I am really relieved that we are here and that someone is watching her closely. Also, we are very happy to get all the messages. They are an encouragement to Evelyn. We realized yesterday that she has been having fevers for over a year. Can you imagine feeling like you have the flu for that long?

April 4, 2008, 4:10 p.m. — Evelyn

Hi. I feel better after getting warm and taking a good nap. I did not sleep well last night. The room felt dry, and I kept going down the hall for a drink of water until I couldn't have anything after midnight. The problem is that what goes in must come out. I almost never sleep well the first night in a new place.

Kevin Guest House is a large old house about a block from the hospital. We are on the second floor, and the stairs are narrow. With my swollen feet in my men's size ten moccasins, I had to turn my feet sideways to climb the stairs. Thank God for railings and Wayne following close behind me.

Another reason I did not sleep well the first night was that Wayne had pointed out a bullet hole in the bedroom window. We had been warned that downtown Buffalo was a dangerous place to go out at night. Sirens blared all through the night. We were not used to the noises of a large city.

We will be in Buffalo for over four months, so Wayne decided to get a mailbox at the closest post office near us. It is about a mile away, and Wayne walks there every day. After walking up on a drug deal the first day, he soon found the safe streets to walk. There is a shared kitchen here at Kevin Guest House. I told Wayne a bowl of cereal would be enough for me the next morning.

The procedure was not bad. The waiting was the worst part. It seems to take a long time to get anything done at a medical facility. I am sure you all have had this experience.

Wayne started his caregiver training today, flushing two of my three lumen lines. He also has to learn to connect infusion pumps, hang medicines, and set the pumps to distribute the medicines at the correct rate.

April 5, 2008 6:55 p.m. – Wayne
Everything went well with Evelyn's checkup this morning. She will be admitted at 7:00 a.m. for the transplant. When she comes out of the hospital, she will have a new immune system.

April 6, 2008, 11:49 a.m. – Wayne
Evelyn had the first of five chemo treatments this morning. She did not sleep last night. Of course, they have stopped the Tylenol and Bupropion, so she is having serious chills and a lot

of pain in her legs and feet. When I left, she was resting but not sleeping. She appears to be very weak and exhausted.

April 6, 2008, 5:10 p.m. — Wayne

I left Evelyn in her room about 5:00 p.m. She was in better spirits. They now have orders to give her Tylenol if her temperature goes above 102 degrees. The doctor also gave her a shot of anti-inflammatory drugs, which he thinks will help with the fevers and the swelling. The swelling has gone down slightly since yesterday, but her legs and feet are still very painful. This is probably due to previous chemo. She didn't eat any lunch, but I hope she will eat dinner since she is more relaxed. I know she is worried about the donor completing the harvesting of the stem cells. I am sure that when the transfusion is over on Saturday, she will be able to relax a great deal.

April 7, 2008, 7:46 p.m. — Wayne

Evelyn had a much better day today. The swelling has gone down in both her hands and feet. She has had a fever, but at 4:30 p.m., her temperature was normal. The NP explained that the fever is caused by the cancer and not the chemo. The pain and swelling are caused by the chemo and may not completely go away. The chemo they are using for this procedure is more potent than any Evelyn has had to date. They can use it because they are not worried about it causing damage to her bone marrow or immune system, since she will build a new one when they infuse the donor cells.

The doctor also wrote an order today to allow Evelyn to decide when she needs to take Tylenol. He said that she was aware that once the fever starts it needs to be hit with drugs immediately, and Evelyn knows when she needs the drugs. He added, "You guys have been managing this for over a year and know better than we do how to take care of her."

This boosted our egos and made us feel as though we were part of the team and that what we thought mattered. Evelyn had a transfusion this morning because her blood counts were low. That gave her more energy. Her voice is coming back, and she has been walking. Each walk around the hallway of this unit equals 1/33 of a mile. She did twenty-two laps today. She also had PT and OT in to work with her today. They explained that the patients who exercise go home earlier and much healthier than the patients who don't exercise. Now she will expect me to keep up. Sunday, I thought I would need a wheelchair to get her the hundred feet from the car to the registration desk for admission.

The chemo she will have on Wednesday and Thursday usually makes the patient sick, but Thursday will be the last day of chemo. Friday is a rest day, and Saturday is the transplant date. Most people are very surprised that she has been taking chemo for almost a year. I am really proud of her. The cards and messages mean a lot. She keeps the printed copies on her tray.

April 8, 2008, 6:42 p.m. – Wayne
Evelyn is doing well today. No fever at all! This is what they told us to expect after two or three days of strong chemo. Today she did thirty-three laps, the equivalent of one mile around the transplant hall. Everyone is taking great care of her. Today, in addition to the regular team of doctors, the head of the department was in to see her three times. This is his week off, but he was here to check on her. They are already getting her ready for recovery. Today, she had physical therapy, occupational therapy,

a nutritionist, a chaplain, and others in to talk with her.

Last night was not a good night. She had fluid in her lungs and swelling around her throat, making it very difficult for her to breathe. It was scary for both of us. The doctors finally got it taken care of around 12:30 a.m. This is the second time this has happened during chemo. The first time was when she took ICE at Bassett hospital in Cooperstown. I think today is the first day since April of last year that she has gone a complete day without a fever. This is still cancer. One minute she is doing great, and the next they are scrambling to help her breathe. However, it seems like the good times are happening more often. Tomorrow she starts two days of a new chemo drug that has the reputation for causing nausea. After that, she is done with chemo.

April 10, 2008, 7:53 a.m. – Wayne

Evelyn had a slight fever spike Tuesday night of 102 degrees, but none Wednesday or Wednesday night. No fevers, chills, or sweats—a great improvement. The swelling in her feet has gone down, and she is wearing a pair of slippers that we bought just before we came to Roswell. She could not wear them before because of her swollen feet. She is still retaining a lot of fluid, but they are pumping a lot of saline with this chemo in order to keep the kidneys flushed. At times, she has had ten different IV bags on her pole.

Evelyn was not sick with the chemo yesterday! Not at all! She was very sleepy and a bit loopy because of the anti-nausea drugs. We are both encouraged. Hopefully, today will be the last day she will ever have to take chemo drugs. She has Friday off, and then Saturday is the transplant. The transplant is an infusion of donor T-cells administered through an IV. It will take about an hour. Ben and Yolanda are here for a few days and will be here on Saturday to lend their support. It is always great to see friendly, familiar faces.

April 10, 2008, 6:56 p.m. – Wayne
Today was a good day. Evelyn had her last chemo and no ill effects. No fevers, no chills, and only a slight sweat for the last twenty-four hours. She did have a couple of scary episodes of not being able to breathe due to the excess fluid. Her feet and hands are not as swollen, but her abdomen is extremely bloated. The doctors expect to be able to eliminate this tomorrow. They are giving her large amounts of fluid to flush the dead cancer cells and to flush out the chemo before infusing her with the new cells.

Last night, one of her blood cultures came back positive for infection. She is receiving three types of antibiotics by IV to fight this infection. Now, she has no immune system. Her white count is zero. From what we see and what the medical team says, she is well on track. She has a great attitude, and I cannot say enough about the great care she is getting.

April 11, 2008, 12:26 p.m. — Evelyn
Hello, all. I want to say hello and thanks for all the messages you are sending me. Today is a day of rest, and I'm tired, probably from the anti-rejection drugs. Tomorrow is a big day. I just need to get rid of this extra fluid weighing me down. Hallelujah, I just talked to the transplant coordinator, and the stem cells are in flight. Thank God! They should be here tonight, and I will get them in the morning.

PART IV

April 12, 2008: Transplant and GVHD

April 12, 2008, 7:23 a.m. – Wayne

As you can see from Evelyn's update, the cells were harvested on Thursday, shipped Thursday night, and arrived at Roswell between 7:00 p.m. and midnight on Friday. She will be infused sometime this morning between 9:00 and 10:00 a.m.

Kelly called early this morning; we are new grandparents. What a day! Solomon James Chripczuk was born at 12:44 this morning. Kelly and John have a baby boy who weighs seven pounds ten ounces and is nineteen-and-a-half inches tall. Kelly arrived at the hospital at 12:33 a.m., so Solomon is a fast mover.

Evelyn and Solomon will share the same birthday. As he gets all of his shots for the first time, she will have to have hers repeated. The day of infusion is considered to be the second birthday for the patient, since when they receive the new immune system, they have a second chance at life. We are very excited for Kelly, John, and Sophia, and it is special that Solomon was born on the day of Evelyn's infusion. It seems like a special promise of life, health, and new growth. We will update again after the infusion is complete. Love, Grandma and Grandpa.

Evelyn's Reflections:

I found out later that Kelly and John had wanted to come to Buffalo for the infusion to be with the rest of the family, but she found out her insurance would not cover the birth of her baby if she traveled so close to her due date. As much as I would have loved for her too be there, I am glad she was home to have her baby boy. All things work out when we put our trust in God.

April 12, 2008, 11:24 a.m. — Wayne

The infusion is over. Evelyn did well. Because of the need to continually flush dead cells from her system, the doctors increased her IV fluids, causing her lungs to fill and making it very hard for her to breathe. Her heart rate went through the roof, causing some tense moments. She went into atrial fibrillation, and I was asked to leave the room for a few minutes. But it is done. She has a catheter and is taking a diuretic to help flush the fluid out quickly. She is sleeping now. When I was asked to leave the room, I was very glad that Ben and Yolanda were here, because it would have been tough to be alone. The stem cells looked like tomato soup. I told her it was not the store brand.

I really appreciate all of your prayers, positive thoughts, and encouragement. I read her messages to her this morning. The bottom line is that all is well here, the infusion is done, and we are on our way to the healing part of this process. Praise God!

Evelyn's Reflection:

Part of this was surreal to me. I do not like having a catheter and asked the nurse if I could get up to go to the bathroom one more time, but it was too late. The tomato soup, as Wayne called it, was hung, and there was no way I was getting out of bed. I don't know exactly what happened, but I remember Ben leaving the room, followed closely by Yolanda. I assumed he did not like seeing me in this situation, and that she had gone to be with him. Shortly, after that, Wayne was asked to leave the room, and there were lots of people going in and out of the room. I had plugs for oxygen in my nose. Suddenly a large oxygen tent was pulled down over me, and the nose plugs were removed. I knew something was going on, but since there didn't seem to be any talking, I did not know what was happening. I was not afraid at any time, but only curious about what was happening.

I witnessed a well-choreographed dance taking place in front of me, as people I did not know waltzed around the room taking care of my problems. I later found out that one of the individuals was a NP from cardiology, and some of the others were from pulmonary. A doctor stood by the door and directed the medical team as if he were conducting a grand orchestra. Soon my issues were resolved, the tent was off, and Wayne was allowed back into the room, followed by Ben and Yolanda.

Later, I found out that my heart went out of rhythm during the transplant. I had to take AFib medicines for about six months. I have never had a problem with heart rhythm again. I also found out that the monitor that is watched at the nurse's station to monitor me was turned off when Wayne stopped there to see what was happening in my room, after he was asked to leave. Thankfully, this whole experience only lasted for a few minutes.

April 13, 2008, 4:21 p.m. — Wayne

This morning, Evelyn looked and acted as good as I have seen her in months. She has not had a fever since Thursday. The catheter is out, and she is up walking. She is on her way to a mile again today. The doctor was in a few minutes ago and said that she was doing A-1. It was snowing a little this morning, but the sun is out now.

The doctor explained what we should expect over the next few days. The anti-rejection drugs, actually a form of chemo, will cause her to have diarrhea, and in a few days, she can expect to exhibit some graft-versus-host disease (GVHD) in the form of sores in her digestive tract. Hopefully, they will not be bad. These sores are a sign that everything is working as it should. The trick is to control them. She is eating supper now and not offering me any.

April 14, 2008, 12:58 p.m. — Wayne

I think I've told you before that Evelyn had a bacterial infection which was being treated with antibiotics. Now the doctors think she has a new one in her blood that keeps returning. It may be caused by the Hickman, or it may be in the lines implanted here on April 4. They took her to surgery to remove the port and the lines. The doctors don't seem too concerned, yet they are in a hurry to get the lines out and clear up the infection. The decision was made to do this an hour ago, and she is already headed for surgery. As of now, she doesn't have a fever from the infection, and I think that is good. I don't really understand how this all works since she is immunosuppressed.

Evelyn was exhausted yesterday after the surgery. Everything went well, and she was back in her room after an hour and a half. She has been taken off a ton of drugs that were affecting her emotionally and physically. Last night and this morning she was antsy and nauseated, unable to sleep or concentrate. As soon as she told her nurse how she felt, the nurse brought some medicine to calm her down. It seems fantastic that the doctors are already weaning her off of some meds. It feels as if we are on the other side of the mountain. Evelyn continues to exercise. She has walked her mile today and is itching to get on the exercise bike, but the nurses said to wait a few more days. They don't want her on the exercise bike until the incision from the surgery heals.

I learned that having an infection in the lines is common and that doctors deal with it quickly. I continue to be amazed by the quality of care she is getting here at Roswell. The team is professional and treat her with respect. They listen to us and respond with immediate solutions. We continue to appreciate your messages and knowing that you are here partnering with us in her care. The care pages have been a blessing to us.

Evelyn's Reflection:

I learned about care pages from a chiropractor in Hamilton. She knew an individual who had been through a transplant and shared with me how much care pages helped her family. When I met with the psychologist before my transplant, she asked me how I planned to spend my time in the hospital. One of the things we talked about was care pages. She informed me that Roswell Park had its own system of care pages. Wayne set the system up for me, and it has been an amazing way to keep so many people informed at the same time. We also used this source to ask for specific prayer requests along the journey. I was able to see who was reading the blogs, with many people responding to our messages with words of love, scriptures of hope and healing, song lyrics, and positive thoughts. Wayne has been so sweet to write for me when I haven't been able to think or type. He hand-printed your messages and brought copies to me when I was in the hospital and didn't have a laptop. Later, we printed some of the posts, and I am relying heavily on them to write this book. I believe God inspired us to print as much as we did because the site was taken down, and we lost most of the blogs.

We later learned the psychologist used our care pages as an example of how to use care pages and how they could be a help to the patient and their families and friends.

April 16, 2008, 1:55 p.m. — Evelyn

Hello everyone. One of the transplant team of doctors came in this morning and said I was on autopilot and that everything looks good. She explained what might happen over the next few days as my healing progresses. I am experiencing a little nausea, but the nurses bring me medications when I need them, so it never gets bad. The worst part is the diarrhea, which varies from day to day. The infections are gone, and I do not have to be attached to the hated pole unless I am receiving drugs, allowing me to be free most of the day to walk and move around the room freely. One thing that everyone encouraged from the beginning was activity. The transplant coordinator explained that I would be expected to get up every day, take a shower, get dressed in street clothes, and move around in the BMT ward as much as I could. I could not go outside the ward or to another floor because of germs.

I am so thankful for your prayers, for good professional care, and for a wonderful, patient, handsome caregiver. I felt the Lord impress me last night with how I needed to be praying for other people on my wing of Roswell, because many of them are sicker than I am. Several times the nurses came and told me to close my door until they came back to open it. The next day, there was an empty bed, and the cleaners are cleaning the rooms for a new patient. It didn't take me long to figure out that not all of these people were going home, but I can only hope and pray they are going to their heavenly home.

Wayne is checking into our apartment after 4:00 p.m. today. He is making a grocery list of the things I can eat. Since he will be cooking for me, I hope he will be eating something besides canned chili and bologna. That has been his diet since we have been here at Roswell, partly because he does not want to spend the money to eat out or at the cafeteria, and partly because he does not want to have to cook and wash dishes. At Hope Lodge, where he is staying, volunteers bring in a home cooked meal once a week, so he does get a good meal then. Blessings to these people who give their time, resources, and talents to treat these patients and caregivers with wonderful meals.

The occupational therapist is helping me with a secret project. Watch out, Solomon, as you may be the receiver of this project. This is a way to keep my hands and mind occupied during the long hours of waiting here. I also may learn to knit, so watch out for those wobbly scarves I may be giving as Christmas gifts. Maybe I will stick to doll scarves, saving the rest of you the embarrassment. It is fun to feel productive. Reading is still difficult, as I have a hard time concentrating. It is called chemo brain, and it is real. I am sure I will address this more later.

I wrote this all earlier and with more humor and somehow it all got lost into cyber space. Okay, I cried just a little since it was a long message for me to type.

Keep Wayne lifted up in prayers; he is exhausted today. Living out of a car will exhaust you. He doesn't want to unload our stuff until we get into the apartment, so he is basically taking only what he needs into his room each day.

April 17, 2008, 4:40 p.m. — Wayne

Evelyn had a big day today. Three of her friends from Morrisville came for a visit. That really raised her spirits. It was good to have some folks from home. I took them to the Anchor Bar, home of the original Buffalo Wings, for lunch. The waitress said they thought her friends were Charlie's Angels, one distinguished man and three babes.

Evelyn is still experiencing nausea that seems difficult to control. She threw up last night. I think it came over her so fast she did not know what was happening. The nurse was very efficient and caring in helping her get cleaned up. I am convinced that she could not be in a better place. The apartment where I am staying is just a block away. It was nice to walk over here in five minutes. I really feel like a different person knowing I will be in one place for a while and have my own space.

Evelyn's white count is now zero, which is where the doctors want it to be, but it also means she is extremely susceptible to infection. The nurses are being very cautious and are leaving her hooked to her IV at all times to avoid any contamination from hooking and unhooking the lines. She is doing well.

Evelyn's Reflection:

I threw up only once, but for some reason I felt awful calling the nurse to clean the mess. I did not have time to grab a bowl or even lean over to protect myself or the bedclothes. The nurse offered to help me take a shower, but I was too weak, so I asked her to wash my legs and feet off and help me change into a clean gown. She had to change the sheets also, but she was very efficient, as most nurses have that procedure under control.

I had to deal with a lot of diarrhea, but I was able to get to the bathroom even while maneuvering the pole. One time, I was not able to get my undies down fast enough, and there was a mess. Normally, I would have thrown the underwear out and used clean ones after washing. This pair was new. So, I pulled on gloves and used my diaper-rinsing skills to remove the worst and then washed them thoroughly in the sink bowl. I hung them to dry and then put them in the laundry that Wayne did for me on a regular basis. The reason I am including this rather personal and gross story is that this was my small rebellion. The doctors would not even let patients use regular toothbrushes because patients' gums get soft and bleed easily. We had to use soft, spongy material that was attached to a handle like a popsicle stick. This is not a good description, but you get the idea. There was not much normal in our life. Once, the head of the department, who was my attending doctor, walked in and caught me cutting my toenails with a regular toenail clipper. He cautioned me to be careful and suggested I always cut my toenails as soon as I got out of the shower, while they were soft from the hot water. I still do that to this day. I was not allowed to shave my legs, unless I used an electric razor. Thankfully, the chemo took care of the hair, and I never did have hair grow back in some areas.

After three weeks in the hospital, I learned a lot of little tricks to avoid infection. Washing the underwear was my most egregious infraction, but there was one night when I had a verbal fight with one of the nurses who wanted to take my Life Savers candy from me. One of the worse side effects of the whole process was an awful taste that I continued to have in my very dry mouth. I asked Wayne to bring me some hard candies that I could suck on, to help with the taste and the dryness. Life Savers was one of those candies. The nurse was afraid I would choke on the candy. I had always slept with cough drops in my mouth since childhood. I was determined that she would not get my Life Savers from me. After a short struggle, she proved to be stronger than me. Looking back, I think I probably looked and acted like a two-year-old, but I also knew my uncharacteristic actions were because I felt as if I had no control over any part of my life. At that point, everything had been taken away from me. After the nurse took the candy from me, I felt defeated.

April 18, 2008, 5:02 p.m. – Wayne

Evelyn has been down emotionally and physically today. Part of the reason is her low counts. Saturday she will begin shots to increase her white count. In about another week we should begin to see some improvement in her white count, and then she should begin to feel better. Otherwise, I think she is doing well. With all that she has been through, I am amazed that she does not have more down times. We walked some today, and I expect she will finish her mile before the day is over. She makes me push her pole now. I think that is cheating or at least spousal abuse!

She ate most of her supper tonight, so the nausea is getting a little better, and the Imodium is working. Today she had what I think will be her last chemo/antirejection medicine. Her stomach should begin to settle down.

April 20, 2008, 8:36 p.m. — Wayne

Evelyn gave us a scare tonight. She was talking on the phone to her brother, and after she hung up, she sat up on the edge of the bed and said, "I don't feel well!" I helped her to the chair, and she said, "I can't breathe!" By the time I let the nurses know, in about fifteen seconds, she was having serious problems. This was very frightening, and she said, "I feel like I am drowning." Her lungs had filled with fluid, and her hands and arms had turned blue. It took about forty-five minutes to get her stabilized. Even though she has had the transplant, she is now in a battle for her life. I am extremely proud of her and the battle she is fighting.

The nurses have inserted a catheter, have put her on 100 percent oxygen, and have given her large amounts of a diuretic. Finally, she is sleeping peacefully and soundly. I am so glad we are in a place that has such a skilled, compassionate, and knowledgeable medical team.

Evelyn's Reflection:

This was one of two nights that Wayne stayed in the room with me. Usually, the doctors don't like for caregivers to stay with the patients. They make exceptions for children and seriously sick patients. It is important for the patient and the caregiver to both get good rest. A couple of times, when I was upset, the nurses made an exception to the policy because they knew I needed the support, and Wayne did not want to leave me. There is a chair in each of the rooms that pulls out into a chaise lounge. The nurse brought Wayne a pillow and a blanket. He did not sleep much because he did not have his CPAP, but that night we needed to be close to each other. Once he knew I was breathing and resting well, he left early and went back to the apartment to sleep.

One other time, the nurse called him to come because I was having trouble breathing. He was staying at Hope Lodge this time. The manager at Hope Lodge sets a security code at 9:00 each night, and no one can come or go without telling her so that she can turn the security system off. Wayne forgot because he was in a hurry to get to me. When he went flying out the door, the alarm went off. Everyone came out of their rooms to see what was happening. He felt bad that he had set off the alarm, but also felt he needed to get to me quickly. I am sure he was not the only person who's ever set the alarm off when they received a message to come to the hospital.

April 21, 2008, 3:20 p.m. – Wayne

Evelyn is much improved today. I hope we don't have any more events like that. The doctor explained that they think the lengthy chemo treatments she has had over the past year have weakened her cardiovascular system, making it difficult for it to handle the fluid. She should improve over time, but it will take a lot of time. I think she finished with chemo and the anti-rejection medicines Saturday. Today is a better day.

April 22, 2008, 8:02 p.m. – Wayne

Evelyn received some good news today. The doctor told her that her white count has started to show up. It was a zero, and I don't know exactly what it is now, but she has a white cell count. That means that the donor cells have started to engraft earlier than they had told us; they had not expected her to have white cells until Saturday or Sunday. One more thing to be thankful for is that her body is accepting the donor cells quickly.

The doctors have determined that she has an erratic heartbeat. I am not sure if this was the cause of or related to her fluid problem. It has now been corrected with medication. I intend to find out more about that tomorrow. She has been sleeping soundly all day until about 6:30 p.m. After that, she perked up a bit, but she is so tired that it is hard to understand what she is saying. I don't know if this tiredness is related to her erratic heart or her counts being low or both. Her platelets have been at eleven all day. If they drop below ten, she will have a transfusion. The rhythm problem is just another piece of the puzzle. I am encouraged. We still have a long journey ahead of us, and the danger of infection and rejections are always there, but she is doing very well.

April 23, 2008, 5:15 p.m. – Wayne
Evelyn continues to improve. Her white count is up to three hundred today. It is my understanding that five thousand to ten thousand is normal. She is still tired. It is an effort for her to talk or eat, but she is much better than yesterday and definitely much better than when she was admitted. The doctor indicated that she may be ready to leave the hospital the end of next week. However, he cautioned not to get too excited. At any rate, she is doing well.

April 24, 2008, 10:28 a.m. – Wayne
Today, Evelyn's white count is (drum roll please) 1,316. That is a four-fold increase over yesterday. She is doing phenomenally. She had a couple of problems over night. Somehow, she pulled her lines out of her chest. No damage done, but she will have to go to surgery this morning to have them replaced. Her oxygen

level also dropped during the night. The doctors don't know why. They have put her back on oxygen and are checking to see what caused the drop. The doctors still continue to take her off of drugs. Yesterday, they halved her dose of the drug that fights neuropathy, which is a sensation of electrical shock, or numbness in the hands, feet, or legs caused by long-term chemotherapy. This is encouraging because in some cases neuropathy can be a long-term or permanent problem. The growth drug used to stimulate the white blood count was also eliminated. I just spoke to the doctor and he indicated that they had also eliminated other drugs. He said that fewer drugs should help her feel better and eliminate her hallucinations. All of this is good news and additional pieces of the puzzle. This is not cookbook medicine. These people at Roswell are phenomenal!

April 26, 2008, 7:42 a.m. – Wayne

Evelyn had a rough day yesterday. She felt exhausted and anxious all day. About 4:00 p.m., she was extremely short of breath. X-rays did not show any problem, but by 6:00 p.m., she had a fever of 101.5 degrees and body aches. Antibiotics took care of the fever by 9:00 p.m. The doctors could not find the cause of the infection, but something was brewing. These episodes remind us that she can get critical quickly. She slept well the rest of the night and is looking forward to seeing some friends today.

April 26, 2008, 6:07 p.m. – Wayne

What a difference a day makes. Charlie and Judy Blaas came to visit us. It seemed good to see Evelyn laughing and talking with friends. She feels much better than she did last night. She's said before that her body could not keep up with her mind.

The doctor told her this morning that the blood cultures were negative, so they don't know what caused the fever, but he does not think it was a tumor fever. He also said she could be out of here in a few days.

We have an apartment about one block from the hospital where we will stay until she can go home—about the first of August, when her hundred days are over. On most days, she will spend part of the day in the outpatient BMT department getting bloodwork and being checked over by one of the doctors. She is looking forward to a good night's sleep and some fresh air.

Evelyn's Reflection:
Yolanda sent us these Bible verses in Lamentations that have always been very meaningful to me:

> It is of the Lord's mercies that we are not consumed, because his compassions fail not. They are new every morning: great is thy faithfulness. The Lord is my portion, saith my soul; therefore, I will hope in him (Lamentations 3:22–24).

April 27, 2008, 5:14 p.m.
Evelyn continues to do well. She has a small rash that the doctor thinks might be a fungal infection, so she has a cream to apply to that area. She remains very tired but is improving every day. The biggest problem is not sleeping at night. The doctor told her to ask for a sleeping pill tonight. She does not want to get into the habit of taking sleeping pills but decided that sometimes they are necessary. She also started walking in the hall again today.

April 29, 2008, 6:03 p.m. – Evelyn

I feel close to being my normal self today! Boy, will I be glad to lose this pole. Talk about carrying around extra baggage. I know the pole holds life-sustaining goodies, but if everything could be changed to oral medications, then I could lose the pole. My doctor is talking about letting me go to the apartment on Thursday, so pray nothing else crops up to stop this move.

A doctor told me that only about 50 percent get to leave the hospital at the time they are expected to leave. I immediately told him that I planned to be in the positive 50 percent, and I was. I know he did not want me to be too disappointed if I was not able to leave the hospital when I was expected to leave. I chose to keep a positive attitude during my treatment, and I think it helped me. I am not saying that I did not get discouraged, but my focus was to be thankful.

One thing that helped me keep a positive attitude was a CD player I kept in my room playing hymns and other Christian music. I played it at night to help me relax. The music was a good anxiety reliever for me. My friend, Miriam Cross, is an excellent piano player. She made a CD of her and another lady playing many of the old beautiful hymns that I loved from my childhood. I played that CD over and over. It helped to raise my spirits when I felt down on sad days. One of the night custodians loved my music and told me it reminded her of her childhood. Later, when Wayne was in the apartment alone, he did not have a radio or CD player to listen to while he was in the kitchen working, so I gave him mine. I knew he would not buy one for himself because we still did not know where all of this was going to leave us financially. I told him to take the radio to the apartment. After I gave him the CD player/radio, several people asked about my music and told me they'd loved to come into my room where there was a sense of peace. The hymns were inspiring other people on the floor.

Wayne did not talk to me about his financial concerns because he did not want me to worry about anything but getting well. After forty years of marriage, I knew him well enough to read his mind. The fact that he was only eating bologna and canned chili was a big clue. By now, I was hoping to be getting out of the hospital soon.

I did become lonesome, even though Wayne visited me several times a day. It reminded me of the time when we first got married and lived in a tiny apartment at North Carolina State University. Wayne traveled for his job, and we lived away from family. When I became lonesome, I would walk down to the laundromat and talk to strangers. Since we were in the city of Buffalo, two hundred miles away from our home in Eaton, I was thankful for the busy staff who entered my room and took a couple of minutes to talk to me. Several of the chaplains stopped in to talk as well. There was one older chaplain who stopped in several times. He related to our circumstances since his wife had been very sick too.

I walked one-and-a-third miles today and did exercises with the physical therapist. I have to be able to climb a flight of steps to get into the apartment, so I am working hard on step climbing. I may have to go up a few steps and then rest, but I will get there. I am feeling good physically. My appetite is still off but improving. A good ole peanut butter and jelly sandwich hit the spot tonight. The nutritionist has started putting a popsicle on my plate at lunch and dinner. She said cold food usually goes down better when a person is nauseated. I know that if I do not eat, the doctors will not let me go home. So, I eat half of a peanut butter and jelly sandwich twice a day. In addition to a popsicle, I have lots to drink. One good thing about being in the hospital at Roswell on the BMT floor is that you can have as much ice cream as you want, even in the middle of the night. Yay!

Again, thanks to everyone for all your kind words, love, and support. I appreciate the prayers and all the love I feel from your messages. The nights are the hardest, as anyone who has ever been in the hospital knows. Hopefully, only two more. Yippee!

April 30, 2008, 6:42 p.m. – Wayne

Unless something else happens, Evelyn will be moving out of the hospital tomorrow afternoon. We have meetings and training all morning, and then she is free. She is very tired tonight, as she walked two miles in the hallway and packed everything in the room. She should sleep well.

I went shopping today for the right foods for her. I had lots of horseradish, olives, cold cuts, and chili but was surprised to find different foods on the hospital's recommendation list. I still need a fire hose and a five-gallon pail of air freshener for the apartment before she gets here.

May 1, 2008, 12:17 p.m. – Wayne

The "Evelyn" has landed. She is out of the hospital until 8:00 a.m. tomorrow morning for clinic. She is tired, overwhelmed, and has car sickness from the ride to the apartment. She is amazingly healthier than she was when she was admitted three weeks ago. Her doctor informed us this morning that she would not have been able to have the transplant if one more week had passed before she got the donor cells. There was some doubt even then and some discussion between the doctors over whether she would be able to handle the rigors of the transplant. This is not over by a long shot. She still has at least a year of immune suppression and dealing with graft-versus-host disease. We are on the way. Every day brings improvements, and we are on a new adventure. We were in the apartment, like Ralph and Alice on *The Honeymooners*. I don't know if Norton and Trixie are in the downstairs apartment, but we will find out.

Evelyn's Reflection:

What a long day. Of course, I got up early to shower and doll up as much as I could with no hair. Everything seemed to be happening in slow motion. Wayne came early, as we were both excited about my coming to the apartment. All sorts of people came in to give us final advice—what to watch and when to call the doctor if this, that, or the other happened. The nutritionist came, the pharmacist came, and several doctors and nurses along with the pulmonologist came. Finally, we had all of our instructions and medical paraphernalia, and my lunch came. I was asked if I wanted to eat my lunch before I left, and I said in a too-loud voice, "No!"

While soaring down the halls in a wheelchair, I thought, "No stopping me now!" As Wayne drove up with the jeep, I experienced my first glorious breath of fresh air. I inhaled deeply, smiled, and rejoiced that I was out of the hospital after three long weeks.

We drove to the post office, which was only one mile away, and I sat in the car with my window down as Wayne ran in to check the mail. We did this because once he got me home, he could not leave me long enough to go to the post office. We finally arrived at the apartment, where I labored up the full set of steps, stopping several times to regain my breath. Wayne followed me close behind in case I started to go backward. While I sat in the living room chair, Wayne cooked me an egg and a piece of toast. Soon, he brought that to me with a glass of grape drink. It tasted very good. As soon as I got it down, it came back up with a vengeance.

This started our stay in the little apartment in Buffalo. I finally figured out that if I waited too long to eat and got very hungry, then the food would not stay down. This problem had an easy fix, and I began to keep crackers in my purse.

May 2, 2008, 3:13 p.m. – Wayne

Evelyn had a good night and day. She had a problem with nausea, threw up twice, but is doing well now. I ran the infusion pump with magnesium for her today and flushed her lines with heparin, and she is still alive. This morning at the clinic, we went over all of her medicines with the nurse, changing the dressing on her Hickman, and programing the infusion pump. I dropped a $1,500 bottle of red medicine, and it smashed all over the floor. The nurse did not say anything, but her face told the story. I think this will go on my permanent record. Evelyn has nineteen different prescriptions. Some of them are taken three times a day. I think the doctors are getting her ready to eat bugs on the Harley! Again, I cannot say enough about the staff here. They are patient, caring, and knowledgeable. Just fantastic professionals.

This afternoon we walked to the corner and back and sat on the porch swing for thirty minutes. I told her that if she is good, I will make her a peanut butter and jelly sandwich for supper.

May 4, 2008, 5:21 p.m. — Evelyn

I am improving daily, but the doctors and nurses have me paranoid, thinking of all the things that could go wrong. I know they are trying to make us take things seriously, but I am not a person who needs the seriousness of the situation pointed out to me over and over. I am always nervous when I go to the clinic and sometimes have to take an anxiety pill, especially if I am having tests. I think I am afraid that there will be a reason for the doctors to keep me. Here is a funny sidenote. Today, one of the doctors shared how hard it is for him to take just one pill. He shared how his patients are his heroes because we have to take up to fifty pills a day. It is not unusual for him to carry a pill around in his pocket for half a day as he tries to get up the nerve to take it. This story intrigued me since he was not one who usually shared from his personal life. I hope he never gets sick. I had a hard time taking so many pills, but I learned to take just a few at a time with a lot of water. I also have a lot of liquid medicines to take and sometimes they are harder than the pills.

Nurse Wayne has learned to give me magnesium with a portable pump, and Tuesday he has to demonstrate his ability to change a sterile bandage. I know he can do it. He is cooking dinner now.

It was too cold to walk today, and since I was not at the clinic very long, we went to the grocery store. I sat in the car while he grabbed a few groceries. He is not supposed to leave me for more than fifteen minutes, and we are required to be within fifteen minutes of the hospital at all times. Another thing: I have to get used to the mask. I feel as if it is smothering me. If I stay in the car, I am away from other people's germs, and I do not have to keep the mask on. We are doing well but would appreciate prayers that neither one of us will get sick.

May 6, 2008, 6:09 p.m. – Wayne

A new problem arose today; Evelyn's blood cultures indicated her body is forming a defense against a virus (CMV) which is found in soil. That does not mean she has the virus, but something is amiss. The virus can cause serious vision problems. Now she has a new IV medicine with a new style pump to learn to program.

The prescriptions are delivered to us at the apartment. I learned to program the new infusion pump. Now when her pole beeps, it is my duty to fix it. No calling the nurse. At 5:00 p.m., she had a slight fever. We called the BMT clinic and then rushed over before the doctor left, and we had more cultures drawn. We can't afford to take a chance since she is immune suppressed. I am afraid that my diverticulitis is acting up as well, and I feel lousy. If I don't feel better in the morning, I will find out where I can see a doctor. This is a hard day, but these are small problems which will pass.

May 7, 2008, 6:43 p.m. – Wayne

Evelyn has an additional antibiotic plus an additional magnesium pill. I also got the name of a walk-in clinic that I can use, if necessary. Our friend, Miriam Cross, came over for a visit today, and she was a real blessing. Just having someone else here takes a load off me, and I was able to enjoy a much needed four hour nap. Miriam, we both enjoyed your visit, even if we did sleep through most of it.

May 8, 2008, 3:35 p.m. – Wayne

Evelyn had minor surgery today to install a new Hickman. This one should stay in for the duration. This is her fourth Hickman. The first one got infected, the second one she pulled out in her sleep, the third one was temporary, and this is the last one, we hope. We get to skip clinic tomorrow and plan to sleep late. Everyone keeps telling us that Evelyn is doing exceptionally well. Next Thursday, she will have a bone marrow biopsy and a PET scan to confirm that the donor's cells have engrafted as the bloodwork indicates.

May 9, 2008 9:19 a.m. – Wayne

Kelly and her family are here. They came for Mother's Day. It is the first time we have seen Solomon. He is almost a month old. We enjoyed getting to meet our new grandson and spending time with the rest of the family. Not going to the clinic today felt like a snow day! Now that Evelyn is retired, I will miss her celebration dances performed early in the mornings when she received the call for a snow day. If only the students knew. Tomorrow we have to go to the clinic and can then spend the rest of the day with the children.

May 11, 2008, 2:01 p.m. – Evelyn

We had a fun day with Kelly, John, and the grandchildren this weekend. They stayed at a hotel nearby and ate their meals with us. I sat in the car and waited while Wayne did the shopping. It is hard for me to sit and watch him do almost everything. All I am allowed to do is fold laundry and put the dishes up after they dry. I am learning to operate the pumps and am comfortable with the fanny pack one, which I need to wear five hours daily to infuse magnesium. I need to learn to program the large pump on the pole. I use this pump twice daily for an hour to dispense an antiviral for the CMV virus. Tomorrow I find out if the CMV virus is negative. It has to be negative two weeks consecutively before I can stop the antiviral medicines. The picture of me sitting in the kitchen holding Solomon shows how strong I am becoming. Thanks to you all for your continued support.

May 12, 2008, 6:33 p.m. – Wayne

Evelyn was scheduled to have a transfusion today. It was put off until Wednesday, since her blood counts are improving on their own. Her bloodwork this morning showed some signs of graft versus host disease, indicating the new immune system is fighting any leftover cancer cells. Our friend Miriam will stay Friday and Saturday night so that I can attend graduation. Evelyn has been training herself to flush the lines, hook and unhook the bags, and program the pumps. Hopefully, I will have everything organized when Miriam gets here. There is a home health service that can come if Evelyn needs help with the pumps. We will ask them to come Saturday to change the dressing on her Hickman lines since Evelyn would have to do it in a mirror. Thursday, Evelyn is scheduled for a PET scan and a bone marrow biopsy to check her one-month progress. It will be a long, tiring, and stressful day for her. At least they have promised to use conscientious sedation after her bad experience last time.

Evelyn's Reflection:

The last bone marrow aspiration was horrible. Two nurse practitioners were assigned to do the procedure. They gave me a lollipop with a mild sedative coating and a local anesthesia to help relieve the pain of the needle going into my hip. The medicines did nothing to help me. They tried to get a piece of bone but were unable to get one to break off. It felt like they were digging on a nerve. I began to cry but did not know I was crying loud enough for the people in the other rooms to hear me. Soon the door burst open, and the doctor yelled, "Stop!" The nurse practitioners had not gotten a piece of bone, but the doctor told them to just use whatever material they had. The doctor went to the waiting room and brought Wayne back with him into my room to calm me down. It took Wayne awhile, but I was finally able to gain control. That was the most awful experience I had during the whole transplant protocol. At the next doctor visit, I declared that I would not have another bone marrow biopsy without conscious sedation. With this procedure, the patient is still awake but has enough medicine to take away the pain and feels only the pressure. I later had one more without conscious sedation, but it was not nearly as bad.

May 14, 2008, 12:31 p.m. – Wayne

We just returned from clinic. Evelyn is exhausted and already asleep on the bed. She had a blood transfusion this morning since she is still anemic. Her bloodwork also showed that she is still positive for CMV.

She needs two negative tests in a row before she can eliminate that pump with the antivirus medicine. This medicine hangs on the pole, making it hard to move around the apartment. Her magnesium also had to be increased to six hours a day, but the backpack pump for it does not interfere with mobility.

May 17, 2008, 7:43 p.m. – Wayne

Well, I am back from Morrisville, and Miriam is on her way home. She took excellent care of Evelyn. Thanks to Miriam for being willing to take care of Evelyn so I could attend graduation. I ran a pair of pliers through the dishwasher to enable Evelyn to open the Heparin in order to flush the lines. Her hands are not very strong. Using the plyers makes giving herself medicines much easier. She also wrote down step by step how to program the pumps. The apartment is so clean it might take me two weeks to get it dirty again. Evelyn looks better than she did when I left on Friday. It is amazing to see her daily improvements, and it was good for me to have a little time at home.

May 19, 2008, 10:05 p.m. – Evelyn

We got marvelous news from the PET scan. There was no evidence of disease. Hallelujah! Praise God for his mercies. We will not hear from the BMB until we go back next Thursday. I am expecting a good report from that also.

May 20, 2008, 6:06 p.m. – Wayne

Today started out well. We went to a fabric store so that Evelyn can make a fleece blanket for Sophia, like the one she made for Solomon. We also did a little grocery shopping. Tonight, Evelyn is exhausted, her legs are hurting, and she is ready for bed as soon as she finishes her infusion. We were in the stores for only a few minutes, but her stamina is low. We also ate later than usual, and therefore she was very hungry. She quickly ate more than usual and threw it all up. We are learning what she can tolerate daily. Tomorrow, we will take things a little slower and eat on time.

May 21, 2008, 5:00 p.m. – Evelyn

I learned the hard way yesterday that I have to eat small amounts at regular intervals, just like baby Solomon eats. In so many ways, this is like being a baby again. I have to explore and find my way. I will have to have all of my immunizations repeated. Today was too cold for me to go out. I find I get cold more easily since I had the transplant. The prediction is for a nice weekend, and Wayne's brother and mother are coming to see us for a few days.

Tomorrow, I find out the results of my bone marrow biopsy (BMB) and also if my Cytomegalovirus (CMV) is negative. Pray it is negative so that I can get rid of this pole that is following me around everywhere like a tall, skinny shadow. Today, I started to work on Sophia's fleece-tied blanket. It is a late birthday present for her. I chose a funny monkey pattern for her. I know she will love the blanket. This craft is something I can do here to strengthen my hands and help the time pass.

Except for the pain in my legs from muscle loss, I felt good today. I need to get out to walk more to rebuild my leg muscles. Wayne walked several times today. He walked a total of five miles. He just walks around the block so that he is always within ten minutes of me. With the cellphones, I can call him if I need help, and he can be here in a matter of minutes. Thank you for your prayers. I know God is hearing and answering them.

May 22, 2008, 10:15 a.m. – Wayne

Evelyn got some excellent news today. Her BMB came back clean. She is now officially in remission. That means no evidence of cancer, microscopic or otherwise. Her CMV test also came back negative. One more negative CMV test, and we begin eliminating the IV pole and the big pump.

May 23, 2008, 7:44 p.m. – Evelyn

Today there was more sun, and I was able to walk around two blocks twice. I had wanted to go a third time, but I knew it would be too much. I finished Sophia's blanket and will mail it next week. I made the bed today also. Yesterday was exactly one year from when my GP told me he was almost sure I had lymphoma. Upon reflection of this year, I am so humbled and thankful that so many friends and family have held me before the throne of grace in prayer. Many people who don't even know me personally have joined in these prayers. That is what the people of God do. I go to clinic on Sunday. We have company on the weekend and also on Tuesday, so we will not write for a few days.

May 29, 2008, 5:10 p.m. – Wayne

Evelyn's CMV test came back negative. Now we can cut the antiviral medicines to once a day. If she stays negative for two more weeks, we will be able to stop this infusion. Now we go to clinic only twice a week.

June 3, 2008, 5:12 p.m. – Evelyn

It is wonderful to go to the clinic only twice a week. This schedule gives us time to do lots of other activities. As the weather gets warmer, we will walk more and build up my stamina and leg muscles.

Wayne has decided to retire and sent in his letter of resignation yesterday. This was a hard decision for him, but the doctor told him I would continue to have lots of doctor appointments and possible problems with GVHD for some time. We decided whatever time we had, we wanted to spend it together. Yesterday, we went to see a movie matinee to help pass some of the extra time we have. I had already spent three hours at the clinic that morning, so I ended up over-doing it. I had a shot to increase my white blood count while I was at the clinic, and it caused my shoulders and hips to ache. My goal for this week is to be able to attend church. About two hours out of the apartment is enough for me. I am still improving my stamina but get tired and overstimulated quickly.

June 5, 2008, 3:59 p.m. – Evelyn

We crossed a new threshold today. We went out to eat at a Ruby Tuesday. I have a lot of rules about eating and am on a low microbial diet. That means no salads, and no fruits unless they are cooked. All foods I eat have to be well-cooked, and I drink only purified water. I carry water and crackers with me in a small cooler bag so that I don't have to worry about getting too hungry. I also have to be very careful of sun exposure, and since it is getting very hot here, we have to find places for me to walk out of the sun. We have walked at the mall several times, a place that works well because I can sit down when I get tired. We still continue to walk outside but must wait until the sun starts to set.

June 6, 2008, 3:01 p.m. – Evelyn

At clinic today, the nurse practitioner said that if I was in the Olympics, I would score a nine out of ten. That sounded great to me. Next week, I will start to wean off some of the meds. Pray that my body and the donor will stay balanced.

June 9, 2008, 8:29 p.m. — Wayne

Today is day 60 out of 100 that Evelyn needs to stay in Buffalo. She stops taking one of her immune suppressants today. This is a big change. It is exciting but also scary. A young man in the Kevin Guest House apartment next to us passed away today after having the same transplant that Evelyn had. It was sobering.

Evelyn's Reflection:

Our pastor called to tell me about the young man who died in the apartment next door. He was concerned the news would set me back. Of course, we already knew. Wayne had talked briefly to the young man's mom at the office when they were checking out.

While it was a shock and I felt compassion for them, I knew better than to compare myself to other patients. Every patient is different, even when they share the same disease and treatment. I knew from the beginning that this was a risky procedure. I had faith that I was in God's hands and that he was in control. I never thought I was going to die, and neither did Wayne.

June 12, 2008, 6:30 p.m. — Wayne

We have had visitors come from Morrisville today, and that helps us pass the time, have other things to focus on, and give us a broader perspective. At the clinic today, the doctor reminded us of how sick Evelyn was when she came into the hospital. This helps keep everything in perspective. She has finished the antiviral, and the pump was picked up tonight. She said she felt joyful when the pump exited our apartment and was loaded in a van to be returned to the hospital.

June 15, 2008, 5:32 p.m. – Evelyn

We escaped the city of Buffalo today for a few hours and drove to the American side of Niagara Falls. It felt inspiring for this country girl to see open spaces and trees for a change. We left the skyscrapers and paved city behind. It was a beautiful day, and the falls were magnificent. The great power of the falls is just a drop in the bucket of God's power.

June 16, 2008, 5:19 p.m. – Evelyn

For the first time today, the doctors and nurses talked about my going home. I still have over four weeks before I can go. I have diligently been marking the days off my calendar. The doctor explained that I would have my restaging between days ninety and one hundred. That will include another PET scan and the hated bone marrow biopsy (BMB). I can also leave the fanny pack magnesium pump off and see how my next bloodwork looks. Things are moving quickly now, and I am trying not to get too excited, because a month is still a long time to wait to go home.

June 19, 2008, 3:43 p.m. – Evelyn

At the clinic today, I was told that I needed to come only once a week unless I had a problem. This is a big step and feels like a step toward freedom and normalcy. I was also advised to make an appointment with my oncologist at Bassett Hospital in Cooperstown. After I go home, I will alternate between seeing my oncologist there and coming back to the clinic at Roswell. I do need to continue the fanny pack pump dispensing the magnesium for one more week and then try alternating days. Today is day seventy, and each day brings me closer to home.

July 2, 2008, 5:51 p.m. – Evelyn

Thank the Lord I made it to another birthday. I turned fifty-nine today and am happy to be alive. We had a visit from my brother, Mike, and his wife, Jackie, yesterday, and now we are waiting for Kelly, John, and the children to arrive. Having company helps to make the time go faster. In other good news, I found out that I may be eligible for a grant which will help with some of our expenses. God has been faithful to provide for us in many ways.

July 3, 2008, 6:41 p.m. – Wayne

We immensely enjoyed Kelly's family visit. We got to explore downtown, with Sophia enjoying playing on the monuments and Solomon happy to be outside in his stroller. We had a small setback at the clinic today as Evelyn's bloodwork showed evidence of the CMV virus. Tomorrow we have to return to clinic at 8:00 a.m. to get more bloodwork and start the ganciclovir again with the large pump and pole. This is her second round with this virus which has serious side effects. The last time, she had to be on the ganciclovir for five weeks.

July 4, 2008, 10:53 a.m. – Wayne

Today at clinic, the nurse explained that it is very common for CMV to return, and as her new immune system matures, it should control the virus. She has a mild case, but we still came home with arms full of medicines, hoses, a new IV pump, and the dreaded pole. This setback will not keep us from going home, but we may need to bring all of this paraphernalia with us.

Evelyn's Reflection:

My friend, the pole, was back again. I would give it a name, but I was afraid it would take that as an invitation to stay forever. At least I had a small break while the children were there.

July 6, 2008, 1:29 p.m. — Evelyn

It is getting hot, so we are staying close to the apartment today. I also have to collect urine for twenty-four hours and keep it refrigerated. I put a large X on the container. I need to take it to the clinic in the morning. I usually have one and half containers, so I am glad I have Wayne as a porter along with all of his other duties. This is not the first time we have had to collect urine. I told him he has carried my urine all over the state of New York. Next week, I have a range of tests to see if I will be able to go home as scheduled. I have a bone density scan, a CAT scan, a PET scan, a bone marrow aspiration, and several others. It will be a hard week, and I appreciate your prayers that all these tests will be normal. We were blessed that Kelly and John were able to stay in a small apartment below ours. Since we had to go to the clinic both mornings that they were here, it made it easier for us to visit with them. They were able to put the children down for a nap and use the baby monitor to keep track of them. God continues to meet our needs in big and small ways.

July 8, 2008, 7:38 p.m. — Evelyn

Yesterday, I had a nurse visit at the clinic only. I had my ganciclovir infusion (for CMV) and had my blood checked. I feel tired. The nurse explained that the ganciclovir makes the blood counts lower, thus causing more tiredness. Please pray that my magnesium holds since I am taking twelve tablets plus a four-hour infusion daily.

July10, 2008, 3:00 p.m. — Evelyn

I had to have my blood drawn twice at the clinic today. The lab made a mistake on my platelet count, and it looked like I needed a transfusion. Even the best make a mistake once in a while. My platelets are fine. It took a lot of time to sort this out. My magnesium is holding at the low end of normal. Tonight, we get to taper off the immune suppressant also known as FK. This is a time when GVHD can become a problem. In other good news, I got a negative on the CMV test. This is the first in a series of two CMV tests which if negative will allow me to cut the time on the large pump in half. If all goes well with the test next week, we will be able to leave that weekend. We will need to have drugs and supplies delivered to our home. I will still be coming back once a week for a few weeks, and we may be able to get our supplies then.

July 12, 2008, 3:57 p.m. — Evelyn

It is a hot day. I have to stay out of the sun as much as possible. When I go out, I wear a large-brimmed hat and a UV-protective long-sleeved shirt. With the mask I have to wear, I make a lovely picture. I do allow myself to wear capris and lavish the sunscreen on liberally per doctor's orders. Direct sun is one of the triggers of GVHD or rejection. I try to be exceptionally careful. Since we are not spending as much time at the clinic, we have a lot of time to kill. We need a new car, so we have started visiting car dealerships and shopping around. When we get home, we will have already made the choice. At least car dealerships are air conditioned, but the car lots are not.

The death of Tony Snow, the White House correspondent, reminded me that every day is a gift. We get to live it only once. Recently my attending doctor talked about how worried he'd been that I would not make it to the treatment. He said that only one week later and I would have been too sick to have the transplant. He explained that the doctors at Roswell really struggle with whom they should pick to put through this procedure since it is very risky. I thanked him for taking a risk on me. God showed up with the right donor at the exact right time. I thank God daily for my healing and for my gift of Wayne as a faithful and supportive caregiver. I could not have gone through this procedure without him. I continue to be thankful for the love and support from all you who are reading my blog and praying for me. We should be going home in seven days. Yippee!

July 17, 2008, 2:52 p.m. – Evelyn

Thank the Lord! The tests are all done, but we will have to wait for some of the results. I had fifteen vials of blood drawn this morning and all of the bloodwork came back fine. The CMV was negative for the second time. All I have to do is use up the remaining medicine that we have on hand. The magnesium count is up, and we will continue to reduce the immune suppressant by 0.1 percent.

PART V
July 18, 2008: Finally Going Home

The doctor said we could go home today! We will go in the morning because we need to have some medicines delivered first. The delivery is around 6:30 p.m., making us get home too late, because I would need to infuse with the big pump before I could go to bed. We need to be back at the clinic on Thursday at 8:30 a.m. We will drive over Wednesday night and stay at a guest house. After a few weeks, we hope to be able to drive and have clinical all in one day, but now it would be too tiring for both of us. I have to follow the same rules at home for foods, drinking purified water, and avoiding germs. I still have to wear a mask except in our home. I can cook some if Wayne does the prep work. I cannot touch any raw meats, eggs, or vegetables. I cannot have live flowers or potted plants because of fungi in the soils. The CMV virus comes from soils.

People with mature immune systems do not need to worry about germs from soils. One bright spot is that I can start to drive again as long as Wayne is with me. Gradually, I will build up my driving confidence.

A wonderful crew of six ladies (four who worked with me at school plus two friends) came to my house to do a top-to-bottom cleaning. A huge thanks to Pat, Sue, Karen, Judy, Dolores, and Betty. I am very humbled that you were willing to take on my dirt. May God richly bless you for your hard work and servants' hearts. Also, extra thanks to Pat who organized the day and took on some extra jobs. Now it is time to pack. I am sure we have more to take home than we came with almost four months ago.

July 18, 2008, 8:12 a.m. — Evelyn

This will be the last update from Buffalo. Wayne is packing up the cooler with medicines, and we will soon be heading across I-90 East to Eaton, New York. I have to finish my infusion so Wayne can pack the pole and pump in the back of the truck. I am glad we did not plan to go home last night. The medicines did not arrive until 11:00 p.m. We are ecstatic to be heading home and feel truly blessed. I wish you could only see this happy dance.

July 21, 2008, 12:29 p.m. — Evelyn

We have been getting oriented and reorganized here at home. I am enjoying the simple things, like a full-sized sink and re-frigerator. I can look out any of my windows and not see any tall buildings, only trees, grass, and flowers. The first night we were home, there were two fawns outside our window. Yesterday when we opened the door to go out for church, a doe and two fawns were in our driveway. How wonderful it feels to live in the woods with nature all around. I love to see the sunlight filter through the trees. I have always had a love for trees, so isn't it ironic that I married a man who loves to cut them down? But I understand that in nature as in medicine it is essential to cut away the dead so that the healthy can survive and thrive. I believe this is a life lesson.

I have to go back to Roswell on Wednesday for a mammogram, and then Thursday morning we have to go to the clinic. When we have two days in a row, we stay in a motel overnight. It was disconcerting when we arrived home on Friday around 2:00 p.m. and I had a message to call Roswell Park. Some of my test results were back, showing good news. My bones have lost density, which is expected after having prolonged chemotherapy. Vitamin D can help this problem. The BMB results will not be back until Thursday. The NP said there was some uptake on my right breast showing on the PET scan, and that is why I need the mammogram. I picked up my last mammogram test done locally to take for the radiologist to make a comparison. The NP stressed the need to be cautious and follow up anything that looks suspicious. This is the way I will live my life now. Once a person has had a cancer diagnosis, everything needs to be checked for any signs of a relapse or a new cancer growth.

July 22–24, 2008 – Evelyn

We are getting ready to return to Roswell tomorrow. Wayne is ordering medicines and figuring out how and when they will be delivered. We need to return the large pump and the pole as I finished the ganciclovir last night. We also picked up our new car today. That took a few hours, and now I am resting while Wayne does laundry. The doctors at the clinic do not want me to wash laundry, but I can fold it and put it away. I am working on organizing all the paperwork related to my illness which started over a year ago.

July 26, 2008, 4:00 p.m. – Evelyn

We are back from Roswell and jubilant that all my tests came back negative. There are no signs of lymphoma anywhere. The only test result we are waiting on is a molecular test to determine the maturity of my new immune system. I continue to tire easily.

July 29, 2008, 5:43 p.m. – Wayne

Evelyn continues to do well. We will update only once a week after we get back from her clinical visits. We need to be careful to protect her from any diseases such as colds, viruses, or fungi. It will be at least a year before her immune system is strong enough to fight these. Now her immune suppressant drugs are being reduced, allowing the donor cells to take over. This is a dangerous time for her if she gets sick. Even a cold can turn into something deadly, at the minimum involving a hospital stay. From now on, it is a balancing act between her own cells and the donor cells.

Aug. 1, 2008, 8:21 a.m. – Wayne

Yesterday, Evelyn went to Roswell in Buffalo (two hundred miles each way) for a clinical visit. Normally, these involve intensive bloodwork, an exam by a nurse skilled in bone marrow transplants, an exam by a nurse PT, and an exam by an oncologist. There is an in-depth review of her drugs, counseling about dry eyes, fatigue, and a whole list of other areas including test results. These things take over two hours and are tiring. Her bone marrow molecular test shows that her bone marrow is 100 percent donor marrow. This is excellent news. Think about this: she is Evelyn with a different person living in her DNA.

The next step is to get her off the immune suppressant. We are at a low dose now, and the bloodwork does not detect it accurately in the blood. Her magnesium infusion has been reduced to once every other day. After she is off the magnesium, her Hickman can come out, eliminating a possible source for infection. The doctors are very pleased with her progress. We were also reminded, according to her blood test, that she is living on the edge since her blood counts are on the low edge of acceptable. Therefore, she is susceptible to infections that would not bother a person with a normal immune system. All good news is celebrated but tempered with caution about possible problems. We choose to celebrate the good but continue to be cautious and protective of her.

August 8, 2008, 8:32 a.m. – Evelyn

At the clinic yesterday at Roswell, I received all good news. I am officially off the FK (Tacrolimus), which is my immune suppressant, and my magnesium count is higher. The FK drug is what depletes the magnesium. Since I am off the immune suppressant now, the magnesium should be stable, at least in theory. I hope to be able to maintain the magnesium by tablet, and then I will be able to have the Hickman pulled August 21.

The doctors will continue to take me off medications as I improve. I saw one of the doctors I have not seen in a while, and he was ecstatic about my progress. He said I had given him several scares. He also told me that he could see me walking from his office window, and it made him feel happy to see me out walking and following the advice, about wearing a large hat and protective clothing. I ordered some UV protective shirts and wear them religiously.

August 12, 2008, 3:52 p.m. – Evelyn

I received good reports from the clinical visit. However, after several calls between Buffalo and Cooperstown, it was determined that my absolute neutrophils were too low—the part of the blood that fights infection. This could have several indications. Because it could indicate a serious problem, I need to return to Cooperstown to have more bloodwork on Friday. The results then will determine if I need a shot to improve this count. Wayne is excited that he might be trained to give me shots. He is a little too gleeful about this prospect and wants to start practicing right away. He has a big grin on his face. As many of you know, cancer is an up-and-down disease. As long as there are more ups than downs, life is good.

August 15, 2008, 12:29 p.m. – Wayne

Evelyn had her blood labs repeated today at Cooperstown, and the absolute neutrophil counts have improved above normal. She will not need shots or medications presently. We also have had some bills the insurance company has been refusing to pay since February. Our employee relations people at my work have helped us with this. We were able to talk to an advocate at Bassett and are hoping to get some help there. It is hard enough to deal with the disease, meds, travel, and other issues without having to fight over getting bills paid.

August 22, 2008, 10:27 a.m. – Evelyn

After going to Buffalo on Wednesday night, I had my normal clinic visit on Thursday morning and had the Hickman removed just before I left to go home. I was able to see the procedure on camera. I had all the operating room personnel laughing at me when I told them the vein looked like a black hole. The more I tried to explain to them about the show we had watched on TV the night before about black holes, the more they laughed. Because I had only local anesthesia which took a while to take effect, the removal was painful at first. As they laughed, I started to laugh, taking my mind off the procedure. The Bible says that laughter is the best medicine, and I have found that to be true. There were many times when I could not laugh, but the few times I could, it had a healing effect. As they remove the Hickman lines, they have to cut the scar tissue away from where it has become attached to the lines, causing the pulling pain.

I find going to Roswell as well as going to Bassett to be very emotional times. Sometimes I have to take an anxiety pill before I enter the building. I think I remember vulnerable times and negative experiences.

My magnesium remains in the middle of the normal range, and Wayne just dumped the remaining infusion magnesium pouches. I still take twelve tablets daily, but every time I can quit a medicine or an infusion, it feels like a small victory. A couple of my levels are at a low normal range, so I have to be careful not to be around anyone with germs. My platelets are below normal but not low enough to warrant a transfusion. On Tuesday, I return to Bassett for bloodwork and a checkup by my oncologist there. On September 4, I return to Roswell for three appointments. I have the clinic, a dental appointment, and a cardiologist appointment. Thankfully, all of these doctors are in the same building. This is one of the advantages of having treatment at a larger cancer institute with specialists available. It is wonderful not to have to buzz around Buffalo to different buildings for these appointments. I do have to drive downtown for my eye appointments.

Wayne and I still need your prayers, as we feel drained both emotionally and physically today. We had a nice visit with Kelly and her family last week, and Ben's family will arrive later today. Seeing the older children and the little ones gives us a lift and helps me know why the fight is worthwhile.

I am happy that I don't have to flush the lines anymore. After today I will be able to take a pill for my antifungal medicines. All of these changes make my life a bit easier.

August 26, 2008, 8:26 p.m. – Evelyn

Today at my appointment at Bassett, my absolute neutrophils, which fight infection, were in the middle of a normal range. This is great news. My magnesium is holding, and my platelets remain low, but not dangerously low. The platelets control clotting, so they are very important. Most of the other counts were near or in normal range. We had an excellent report, and we are very thankful and happy. This visit was not as stressful as most have been.

The only stressful part was that Bassett had dropped my insurance and therefore had sent the last two visits to Wayne's insurance, which is my secondary insurance. Hopefully, we got it all figured out. If not, we know who to contact. It was a blessed day.

September 5, 2008, 10:45 a.m. – Evelyn

Today at Roswell, I had a dental visit first and a cleaning and found out a couple of my old fillings need to be redone. Chemo is very hard on teeth. I will schedule these on a day when I need to come here anyway.

The bone marrow team thinks I have some signs of GVHD. This is good as long as it is kept in check. I have GVHD on my skin in the form of a red rash, plus other signs in my mouth and lungs. I will need to return to Roswell next week and have a pulmonary function test to see how my lungs are functioning. If there is a problem, I will need a steroid inhaler. The GVHD is mild now, and I will use a steroid cream for my skin. So far, I don't need anything for my mouth. If the GVHD worsens, I will need to go back on the immune suppressant for a while. I postponed my Bassett appointment for now. Roswell will deal with all GVHD issues.

I saw the cardiologist. He took me off the AFib medication but left me on blood pressure medicines. He does not think I will need to see him again unless I have problems.

We continue to praise God for my health and believe for continued healing. The GVHD could be a setback. The doctors were happy that I had some GVHD since it fights against the return of the lymphoma. The donor cells are working hard to destroy any cancer cells left behind. The team at Roswell are very aggressive, staying on top of any problems, and we have great confidence in their expertise. Anytime one of us calls the BMT, we get a rapid response with clear instructions.

We appreciate your continued prayers as we are impatient people who are eager to return to a normal life, but we see how much better I am than five months ago.

Sept 11, 2008, 8:22 p.m. – Wayne

We found out this week that Evelyn does have GVHD (graph-versus-host disease) on her skin, in her mouth, and probably in her lungs. It was interesting to see the reactions of the nurses and doctors, as they were excited to see the GVHD. Having GVHD is a good sign that the new immune system is fighting the lymphoma, preventing it from reoccurring. While we were looking at it as a bad development, they saw it as healing. A rash and sores in your mouth is an annoyance, but if it is causing healing, we can deal with the annoyance. The doctor reemphasized today that Evelyn's cancer was a particularly aggressive type which likes to reoccur. We need to watch this GVHD closely since it can change quickly from mild, to severe, to life threatening. She was prescribed three medicines which all contain steroids. A mouth wash, two creams, and an inhaler should keep the GVHD in check. We are to call if anything changes. We are encouraged that everything is going according to plan. The staff at Roswell Park are on top of things and anticipating things. Evelyn is 200 percent better than she was just a few short months ago. Her lab numbers are improving each week.

September 17, 2008, 12:44 p.m. – Evelyn

It was a pretty drive to Bassett Hospital in Cooperstown today. After the bloodwork, I saw my original oncologist. She was happy to see me doing so well. She went over the bloodwork and gave me a physical. I am doing well and had only a few minor complaints. The main complaint at this time is an awful taste and dry mouth which makes it a chore to eat. I used a mouth rinse that Wayne calls "fake spit," but it made me nauseated. The second problem was worse than the first. I quickly gave the fake spit a no, which disappointed Wayne because he liked to tell everyone about my "fake spit." I should have made him use it. My cough and rash are better. We return to Roswell next Wednesday. I need some dental work and have a clinic appointment.

PART VI

September 25, 2008: Readmitted to Roswell Park for GVHD

September 25, 2008, 2:32 p.m. — Wayne

According to her bloodwork this morning at Roswell, Evelyn's GVHD is becoming an issue. She has a significant amount of GVHD in the form of a rash on her skin and sores in her mouth. It is becoming difficult for her to chew, and nothing tastes right. The doctor has decided to admit her back into the transplant wing. Over the next few days, she will have IV steroids and go back on the immune suppressant. This morning they explained that without some GVHD, her cancer would return. This is not a surprise for the doctors and is actually a part of the healing process. The trick is to keep the GVHD in balance, so they need to be able to watch her. She will be here a few days.

I think she is a bit relieved to be here but also discouraged to think about how fast her health can change. This whole transplant process is a long one, and we will be dealing with it for a long time. It is frightening that we did not notice the severity of the symptoms. We actually thought things had improved. Now she is resting comfortably, and the medicines are being delivered by infusion. I know she is dreading the effects the steroids have on her appearance, and I don't blame her. We hope this is a short-term deal.

Evelyn's Reflection:

I can hardly keep from crying while I read Wayne's message from that day. I knew something was very wrong when I bought an ice cream cone at a rest stop on I-90, and it burned my tongue when I tried to lick it. Ice cream is definitely one of my favorite foods, and to not be able to lick the cone was horrible. My tongue felt like sandpaper. I almost begged the doctor to let me go home and pack some clothes and come back the next day. He would not budge. He said that Wayne could go home and come back, but I did not want him to leave me there alone. He said the hospital would give me a toothbrush and other toiletries and a gown to wear. I wanted to say I had seen their toothbrushes, but I know when I am defeated. I know, in retrospect, that he was protecting me, but at the time it did not feel that way. As fast as GVHD flares, it was not safe for me to wait another twenty-four hours to start the IV drugs to combat this disease.

If we had known how long I would have to stay on the immune suppressant, I am not sure how we would have handled it. Actually, we would have handled it the way we did, because we had no options. I felt so discouraged to be readmitted to the hospital, like a failure. I learned later that all the survivors are readmitted and many more than once. I learned to trust my doctors even more after this short stay. Wayne had to learn to recognize GVHD, along with all of his other responsibilities. As usual, he stepped up to the task.

September 26, 2008, 1:54 p.m. — Wayne

This morning, Evelyn had a PICC line put into her arm just above the left elbow. It worked similarly to a Hickman line. She currently has four infusion bags hung, including steroids. She may try out for Major League Baseball when this is over. The best I can tell, the GVHD is about the same. I am not a good judge, and I have not seen the bloodwork yet. The doctors are surprised that she is not itching and that her mouth is not hurting her worse.

September 27, 2008, 5:28 p.m. — Wayne

Evelyn is improving, and her bloodwork indicates the GVHD is cooling off. Her mouth is still dry and sore but looks better. Her skin does not look better to me, but she is responding exactly as she should. The plan is to begin reducing the steroids tomorrow or the next day and then dismiss her in a few days. She can be released with pills and oral medicines, but the lines will stay in just in case. That means changing dressings and flushing lines again. It is not hard, but it opens a door for infection. The doctor indicated today that we may need to remain in Buffalo for a few days after she is dismissed. This episode has set her back from getting her childhood immunizations. All of her childhood immunizations need to be replaced since her immune system was completely destroyed in order to kill the cancer cells. She will need to be off the immune suppressant for six months or longer before the immunizations can be started. She is responding well, and this is just one bump in an extremely long road.

Evelyn's Reflection:

The immunization dates kept changing as the protocol kept changing over time and with different patients. Some of them I had to repeat several times because they did not work. Titers, which measure the effectiveness of the immunizations, were checked often to see if the immunizations were doing their job.

September 29, 2008, 8:03 p.m. — Wayne

I have been staying at Hope Lodge, and Evelyn will be in the hospital a few more days. Her IV meds need to be switched to oral meds before she can go home. This should happen tomorrow morning, and then her labs need to be watched closely before she can be dismissed. I came home this evening to get some clothes, pay some bills, and check the mail. We did not expect to stay in Buffalo and were not prepared with clothes. I plan to go back first thing in the morning. Evelyn is tired and ready to get out of the hospital. She is in isolation in a small room.

Evelyn's Reflection:

After this surprise admittance to the hospital, I kept suitcases with clothes for me and Wayne in the trunk of the car. We were blessed that we never had to use them. I felt better knowing I would not get caught without a few changes of clothes again.

Being admitted into the hospital over two hundred miles from home without notice set me back emotionally. I think I felt very vulnerable at the time. One of the hardest parts of this ordeal for us was feeling as though we had no control over anything. I am still aware today that God is the only one in control, and I have to continue to trust him in all areas. I always knew this at some level, but now it is much more real on a daily basis.

Sept 30, 2008, 4:52 p.m. – Wayne

Evelyn has only one IV tonight. She should be on all oral meds by morning. If her labs look good, she will be dismissed to Hope Lodge for tonight. Tomorrow, her labs will be checked again, and if all looks well, we will be able to go home in the afternoon.

PART VII

October 2, 2008: Home Again and More GVHD

Oct 1, 2008, 1:23 p.m. – Wayne
Evelyn was dismissed from the hospital this afternoon. We are staying at Hope Lodge tonight and then will go home if her labs are okay in the morning. She will not need to go home with IV drugs but will keep the PICC lines for a while.

Oct 2, 2008, 3:49 p.m. – Wayne
We arrived home this afternoon with several new meds to incorporate into the pill box. I made an Excel spreadsheet for medications to help us keep them straight. The dosage on some drugs has been lowered, and she will not need them long. We will be returning to Roswell every week for a while. We travel to Bassett next Tuesday for bloodwork and to see the oncologist there. Then the next day we go to Roswell for a clinical and bloodwork on Thursday.

Most of the GVHD symptoms have disappeared. Her taste is still off and may be for a while. Evelyn responded well to the treatment, or "tune-up," as the nurses called the short stay in the hospital. She will be restaged, which involves a CAT scan followed by a PET scan. Restaging will take place every three months for the first year.

October 3, 2008, 5:21 p.m. – Evelyn
It is truly great to be home, even on a cold day in October. The leaves are displaying their magic, and there are even a few drops of sleet. I am mostly sorting papers, clothes, and organizing for the fall and winter. After a nap, the sun came out, and we were able to walk two miles in Hamilton. It is imperative that I keep moving so that my joints don't lock up. I saw a former student and a former colleague at the coffee shop. That was a lovely treat. It is nice to be remembered. Now Wayne is grilling some meat because I still can't touch raw meats. I am able to open a can, heat vegetables, and set the table. We are learning to work well together. I am so blessed in many ways to have a wonderful, loving, patient, and talented husband. A friend came and planted fall flowers on Wednesday night. God is good and has surrounded me with great people.

October 9, 2008, 1:30 p.m. – Wayne
We will be spending another night in Buffalo. Evelyn's blood-work indicated her sodium level is extremely low. The nurses are forcing her to eat salty potato chips to increase her sodium. Leave it to Evelyn to have a malady which requires her to have more salty snacks. I am jealous. Force-feeding potato chips does not seem fair. Her liver functions indicate she has GVHD in her

liver. She continues to have a hard time chewing and swallowing, indicating more GVHD in her mouth. This afternoon she will have bloodwork. At 5:30 p.m., she is having a CAT scan.

Oct 17, 2008, 7:42 a.m. – Wayne

I counted last night, and we have been at Roswell in Buffalo or at Bassett in Cooperstown for eighteen of the last twenty-three days. No wonder we are tired. Yesterday was a full day. She had lab work, a full clinical, and then a PET scan in the afternoon. The doctor expects the scan to be clean, and we may hear from it today or Monday. Her bloodwork shows her numbers are improving, especially the sodium and potassium. I guess we can bag (no pun intended) the potato chip diet. Her sugar level was very high, something which can be caused by steroids. They do not want to put her on insulin because it can cause other problems. Now we are on a diabetic diet with lots of red meat. What a life. She is basically on a meat and salt diet. My favorite.

On the way home from Roswell, a BMT NP called and told her she is positive for CMV. I am hopeful the infusion pump and drugs can be overnighted. If not, I will be on the road to Buffalo early in the morning. I am glad she still has the PICC line in place. Her skin GVHD is under control, but she still has some in her mouth and now in her eyes. Yesterday, I counted forty-two pills, ointments, and other medicines she is on daily. In addition, she has eye drops, inhalers, and heparin flushes. Finally, her hair is turning red. Those of you who have seen her lately know that her hair came back very curly. The grey is turning red. Something new every day. We are glad we have a place like Roswell to help us. Her doctor said he could not predict what hair will do.

October 17, 2008, 1:21 p.m. – Evelyn

Hallelujah! I just got the phone call saying the PET scan is normal and does not show any evidence of disease. Everyone, say a great big, "PRAISE THE LORD!" with me. The CMV drugs will be delivered tomorrow. It is not a large pump and pole, but a gadget about the size of a tennis ball which I will be able to carry around in my pocket. I will need to use it twice a day for two weeks or longer until I get two consecutive negative blood tests. Then I will use it once a day for another two weeks. It is one more thing to keep track of, plus the medications have to be kept in the refrigerator. This is better than having twenty-four hours of urine in the refrigerator.

Oct 22, 2008, 9:11 a.m. – Evelyn

We head off to Buffalo again today. It is only snowing a little and should not pose a problem. I do have a few things I need people to pray about: side effects from steroids, insomnia, moon-shaped face, and high glucose. I do not know how much longer I will need the steroids. Pray it will not be long because these symptoms are making me feel discouraged. It is hard to look into a mirror and not recognize myself. This is actually worse than no hair.

October 23, 2008, 6:50 p.m. – Evelyn

All of my numbers are near normal except glucose. I did not eat any sweets this week, so it must be steroid induced. I am starting a low dose hypoglycemic pill tomorrow. I am upset about this since I am the only one in my family that is not diabetic. I need to understand that I cannot control the effects of the steroids. As the steroids go down, the glucose levels will go down. I need to go off the steroids slowly so the GVHD will not flare. This is like walking on a balance beam. One small shift in weight, and the whole thing starts to tumble. I will be using a blood glucose monitoring system twice a day until my blood glucose is normal again.

I have some other steroid-induced symptoms, including muscle weakness in my right hip and leg and neuropathy in my toes and the balls of both feet. I was disappointed to find out that I have to use the IV pole again for the ganciclovir since the neat, handy little ball dispenser was not delivering enough dosage to meet my needs. I will be using the large infusion pump for another four or five weeks. This is mostly an inconvenience. Wayne will be able to attach extensions on my PICC line lumens, so I will be able to unhook myself. At this rate, it will be at least six weeks before I am off the steroids.

I am presently taking at least fifty pills a day, including eighteen magnesium pills. I also use an inhaler twice a day, a liquid antiviral three times a day with my meals, five steroid rinses a day for five minutes each, two steroid skin creams twice a day, flush PICC lines twice a day, check my glucose twice a day, and take an immune suppressant twice a day. In addition, I have to use the infusion pump twice a day. Wayne will have to retrain me on the pump. I can do most of this by myself except flushing the lines. Thankfully he has made a spreadsheet displaying all of this information, including times. He also fills the pill boxes and orders the refills and new prescriptions. I have six additional medications to use as needed. In addition, Wayne offers me great emotional support. No wonder we are both exhausted. Chemo brain makes my memory not as strong as it was. I am thankful I have Wayne to remind me and help me keep all of this organized. We have very busy days. He also does laundry, cooking, shopping, and cleaning. He is a saint.

I was surprised that the doctor suggested we could plan a trip to warmer climates later this year. He had originally said no travel for a year. The nurse laughed heartily when Wayne asked if we could take a motorcycle trip out West in the fall. She even said she wanted to be present when he asked the doctor. We are very naive about the seriousness and length of convalescing this will take. I cannot travel by plane, but we can head South for a short trip around the first of the year. We will need a U-Haul to carry the medical supplies. Thanks for all the prayers yesterday, and I did sleep better last night.

October 30, 2008, 6:26 a.m. - Evelyn
We received ten inches of snow overnight and had to cancel my clinical in Buffalo. When we woke up, there was a large maple tree lying directly across our driveway. Thankfully, it missed the power lines, so we had electricity, heat, water, and lights. Wayne had to remove part of the tree and plow the driveway so we could get out. After that, he took care of changing my sterile dressing, sorted out my pills, and ordered refills for the next week. Next our power went off and stayed off for six hours. We ran our generator to have heat but could not leave the house with it running. It was getting late when I called and told the BMT clinic receptionist that we would have to cancel my appointment and reschedule for the next day. I was feeling very stressed about missing the appointment, but after I rescheduled, I felt better. There are some things we cannot control no matter how hard we try. We left that afternoon after the power came on to spend the night in Buffalo so that I could go to the clinic early the next morning.

At the clinic, we got good news. My CMV test showed a negative, and if the one this week is negative, I will be able to take pills for the remainder of this cycle. Taking pills is easier than an infusion. My glucose is leveling out. I am checking it twice a day and keeping a chart to show the doctors. All of my symptoms of GVHD are better, but I still have aggravating sores in my mouth. My health situation is improving in all areas.

October 31, 2008, 4:32 p.m. – Evelyn

I received good reports today, including the issue I prayed about the most, steroid levels. The doctors continued to lower my dose by a third. Getting off the steroids will help other issues, including sleeping, muscle and joint pains, and tooth decay. My mouth is still sore, and I still need to use the rinse five times a day, but there are no open sores. I am off the glucose medication but will continue to monitor it for a while. The big pump is required for the ganciclovir once a day for two more weeks. I discontinued one drug and reduced the dosage on three others. We will continue to go back to the clinic weekly for a few more weeks. I am thankful that my health is improving and that the drugs are becoming more manageable. I appreciate all of your prayers for my needs. They are working, so keep them coming.

Nov 7, 2008, 4:20 p.m. – Wayne

Thursday, Evelyn's bloodwork looked good, and the steroids are being reduced. It is necessary to reduce the dosage slowly because of the open sores in her mouth. We have about ten more days of ganciclovir infusions, and then we are hoping to be done with the infusions by pump. Once she is off that medication, we will go to Roswell one week and Cooperstown the next. We are at Ben and Yolanda's home in Virginia tonight. We left Buffalo yesterday and spent the night with Kelly and John in southern Pennsylvania. All the grandchildren are growing fast. This is the first time we have traveled to Virginia since last December. Last week, we went to my mom's house in northern Pennsylvania. We decided a few pumps and poles could not keep us from traveling to see family. It felt good to see them all and to resume our normal life, even if we had to carry a cooler full of medications.

November 13, 2008, 5:52 p.m. — Evelyn

Our trip to see the children and grandchildren went well. I was tired and ready to get home by Monday afternoon. Tuesday, we had to run errands, unpack, wash clothes, and repack to go to Buffalo on Wednesday. I am still not allowed to do laundry. When we arrived at Hope Lodge, some of the nurses from Roswell had prepared a wonderful ham dinner for all the patients staying there. I was able to eat most things on the menu and enjoyed a marvelous treat. Wayne was able to enjoy a meal that he did not have to prepare.

Clinic went well. My counts were all close to normal, and my CMV was negative. I was ecstatic to learn that I could go off the pump on Sunday. The next Thursday, my PICC line would be pulled. No more changing the bandages. Wayne did a marvelous job with this, but it always made us nervous. Freedom from the PICC lines and pole will be liberating. The steroids continue to be reduced one week at a time. The doctor reminded us that if I lower the steroids too rapidly, there will be a chance of another flare of the GVHD, causing me to start all over. I am learning to be patient.

We were frustrated when we arrived home and found Wayne had received some returned forms from his insurance company rejecting coverage. He had spent six hours completing them. We were eligible to receive reimbursements from his insurance for our travel expenses to both Buffalo and Cooperstown. The explanation said I was not eligible. He has been fighting this battle since March. We finally received reimbursement for some items in August. The insurance company continues to come up with all types of reasons to say I am not eligible. They even went as far as to say I was not a cancer patient since I had a stem cell transplant. There were constant arguments between my insurance company and his insurance company. My insurance never covered travel, but his was supposed to cover all of our travel for medical purposes. Wayne spends hours on the phone talking to machines trying to get this sorted out. I know it will be resolved eventually, but it is very frustrating and time consuming, especially when we are expending all of our energy on the disease and working to be healthy and strong. The time when they did pay, we were able to get some help from someone in the Attorney General's Office. We may have to go that route again.

After spending hours on the phone when we were staying in Buffalo, I was able to get grant money from the LLS (Leukemia & Lymphoma Society) and another source to help defray the costs of testing for donors. My colleagues at work raised almost a thousand dollars to help us with expenses, in addition to providing some meals. Their generosity and support on the care pages was wonderful and greatly appreciated.

November 21, 2008, 5:47 p.m. — Evelyn
I have mixed feelings about yesterday's visit. The good news is

that I am going to be able to skip going to Roswell next week unless a problem occurs. I can go to my GP in Hamilton for my blood pressure check and some bloodwork on Monday. In addition, I was taken off one medication that was causing my blood pressure to be high. Other blood counts were in the normal range, and a big relief is that we did get to leave the big pump and pole in Buffalo. The disappointment was that I could not get the PICC line pulled. The doctor wants me to keep it in case I have more problems with CMV. I also was not able to go down on my steroids this week because I had some pink in my skin color and new mouth sores. I tried to convince the doctor that the pink was a reflection of the red sweater I wore that day. He did not buy my explanation. These are signs that the GVHD is starting to flare.

Pray for Wayne and I both that we can get the rest we need both physically and mentally on my week off.

December 4, 2008, 5:41 p.m. – Evelyn
I had an excellent clinic today. My PICC line was pulled, taking about one minute with no pain or blood. This is a real freedom from bandage changes and flushes. All of my counts were good. The doctor lowered the steroid levels. I will take different doses on alternating days. On the low dosage days, I may have some moodiness, but nothing I can't handle. If there are no new problems, we will get to skip another week. All of these blessings are answers to prayers.

December 19, 2008, 12:37 p.m. – Evelyn
I am happy to report that I had another excellent clinical yesterday. All of my lab results were excellent. I do have GVHD in

my eyes, and I made an appointment to see an ophthalmologist in Hamilton in January. In the meantime, I will use eye drops to help with dryness. My magnesium was cut back by a third. Over a week, that is a reduction of forty-two pills, from eighteen per day to twelve per day. The doctor also approved a cheaper pill. My wallet is singing a love song. My steroid dosage was also reduced. Every time it is lowered is a step toward normalcy. I was due a CAT and PET scan in January, but I decided to have the CAT while I was here. We had already given up our room at Hope Lodge, so we had six hours to kill. The manager was gracious to let us relax in their large living room space. We finally left Roswell at 7:30 p.m. and arrived home around midnight. I grabbed a nap in the car, but of course Wayne couldn't. We were ahead of the predicted storm that did not arrive until morning. The other option was to go for the CAT on December 26, and that would have put a damper on Christmas. Now I do not need to go back until January 2. I am praying for you, as I know you are praying for me.

Dec 24, 2008, 8:45 a.m. – Evelyn
Wonderful news! I called yesterday and found out my CAT scan results were negative. I saw the eye doctor in Hamilton, and there is no damage or disease from all the chemo I have taken. I will continue to take drops for dry eye. We head into Christmas and the New Year with many blessings and praises to our marvelous God.

January 3, 2009, 8:47 a.m. – Evelyn
Hallelujah! I am entering 2009 healthier than I entered 2008. Although we had some steep hills and low valleys this past year,

God was faithful, and we learned to depend on him more than ever before. I had a PET scan yesterday and will call for the results on Tuesday. I continue to have GVHD in my eyes and mouth. This is a matter of continued prayer. I was able to lower my steroids again, but the rest of my meds stayed the same. All of my counts are normal or close to normal. I do not need to return to Roswell until January 22. This is exciting news and will be the longest I have gone without a doctor appointment in two years.

We are starting to pray and plan for our future and would like your continued prayers that the GVHD would not flare again. Also pray that we would sense God's plan for our future.

January 6, 2009, 1:15 a.m. – Evelyn
I am ecstatic and thankful for a negative report on my PET scan. Praise the Lord!

January 15, 2009, 1:17 a.m. – Evelyn
I did not make it through my three weeks between doctor appointments; however, I was able to see my primary care doctor in Hamilton instead of driving to Buffalo. A cold I have had for a few days seemed to be getting worse and settling into my lungs. The doctor took bloodwork and sent me for a chest x-ray. The bloodwork and chest x-ray came back negative, but the cultures take a longer time to get results. I have another antibiotic to take for ten days. That makes three that I am taking. It seems like overkill, but one thing the doctors and nurses have drilled into my head is how weak my immune system remains and how quickly I can become septic. I have to call in the morning to report how I am doing and will be rechecked on Monday.

My eye GVHD is becoming more difficult to deal with, and I need to find a doctor to put plugs in my tear ducts. My mouth is better.

Feb 3, 2009, 8:30 p.m. – Evelyn

I am now the proud owner of two super duper silicon tear duct plugs. I now understand that the eyes have two sets of tear ducts. One is for crying and the other is to moisten the eyes, keeping them from getting too dry. Think of your eyelid like a windshield wiper: as the eyelid closes, it spreads a film of lubrication over the eye. There is a duct in the top and one in the bottom of both eyes. If the bottom one is plugged, then the moisture will stay in the eye longer. The tears made when we cry are different; they just run out of the eye. I also have another drop to use at bedtime. This makes three drops to use.

I accidently took a high dose of steroids today. If you see someone hanging from a chandelier, it is probably me. Thankfully, my steroids continue to be lowered slowly.

February 12, 2009, 5:39 p.m. – Evelyn

Today marks ten months since my transplant. During clinic today, all my blood counts looked great. My mouth continues to give me trouble, but my eyes are somewhat better with the plugs. I do not need to go back to clinic for a month. This is a really big step, and I feel thankful to be doing well. My steroid use is still going slowly down.

We are planning to take a trip south in a few weeks. Even though I am not out of the woods yet, I have turned a big corner and can see the light.

Feb 23, 2009, 8:36 p.m. – Evelyn

In the morning, Wayne and I are heading south for about two weeks. The car is packed except for a few last-minute items. We plan to stop and see family along the way and then stay in Hilton Head, South Carolina, for a week before heading back. I am low on southern cooking and am looking forward to some sweet potato pie along with other southern specialties. I am also looking forward to seeing my mom, whom I have not seen in a year. We hope to visit all three of my brothers' families as well as Ben and Kelly's family. That is a lot of people, and I pray they are all well.

April 7, 2009, 1:12 p.m. – Wayne

It was exactly one year ago yesterday when Evelyn was admitted to Roswell Park for her pretransplant chemo. To be honest, we were not certain if she would make it to the transplant and had no idea what lay ahead, but we knew our choices were limited. We were uncertain how we would do this financially and even thought we may have to sell our house to pay for her treatment. What a difference a year makes. Last week she had a CAT scan, and the results were negative. There was NED (no evidence of disease). We have other tests to take this week including bone density, PET scan, bloodwork, and a clinical visit.

Our lives still revolve around doctor visits. Last week we had three, including her oncologist in Cooperstown, an eye doctor for more tear duct plugs, a dentist, and a clinical at Roswell Park. We spend a lot of time and concern while waiting for the UPS man to deliver drugs.

Today we are going to the Harley dealer in Utica to get her a helmet with a large protective shield to keep the sun off her face. Yes, I am aware it is snowing, but we have plans for when it stops—probably not a trip to Montana, but there are a lot of local roads we have not explored yet.

April 10, 2009, 1:38 p.m. – Evelyn

We are praising God for a negative PET scan result today. My bloodwork looks good, but I have lost some bone density since July due to the chemo and steroids. I will use medicines and exercise to combat this. One more month, and I should be off steroids.

I continue to know that I am a miracle and that God has planned this out in advance. He was not surprised or frightened by my diagnosis and knew exactly what donor I needed and when I would need her. I could not have gone through all of this without my wonderful caregiver, Wayne, my husband, who was always there for me in every situation offering love, support, wisdom, and stability. I am truly blessed with the doctors, nurses, technicians and all the wonderful workers at Roswell Park Cancer Institute. The support of my family and friends has also been phenomenal. I never anticipated that so many people would read this blog and answer with love, support, and humor. According to my doctors, this is not over and will not be for a long time. We know this but choose to live life as fully as possible and continue to praise God for his goodness.

Evelyn's Reflections:

I started my story on a high note with our trip out West in July 2006, because I wanted all of the readers to know how God prepared us for this cancer journey in 2008, which would have many pitfalls and dark days along the way. When I finished the blog, I had no idea the problems that were still ahead of me.

PART VIII
June 19, 2020: Twelve Years Later—More GVHD Issues

Eyes

My eyes ended up being one of my biggest problems from GVHD. I continued to have tear duct plugs put in, and they continued to fall out immediately. I finally found a doctor in Buffalo who put one plug in surgically at Buffalo General Hospital. I will save the remainder of that story for another time. I have had appointments with ten different ophthalmologists over the past twelve years. Roswell Park Cancer Institute does not have ophthalmologists on their staff, but they recommend specialists nearby. As with most specialists, it is hard to get an appointment to see them.

One ophthalmologist cauterized my tear ducts so I would not need plugs. My eyes grew big as he moved toward them with a red-hot poker to do the cauterization. One of the ducts did not fully close, allowing a bacterial infection to blossom. The doctors at the BMT knew that I needed autologous serum eye drops, which are made from the patient's blood. I could not find an ophthalmologist in Central New York that would agree to give me these drops. Finally, because so many transplant patients had the same problem, the lab at Roswell started to make the drops in-house. After several years of using every type of drop available, over the counter and prescription, plus dozens of plugs, I was finally able to get autologous drops and still use them to this day. This was not a miracle drop, but it did begin to soothe the aching eyes I was dealing with. I still had the eye infection going on even after taking multiple antibiotic prescriptions. We were finally able to find an ENT surgeon in Tampa, Florida, who helped me get over the infection.

It was not easy. I had to have tubes surgically placed in the corners of my eyes, so the fluids drained down through my nose and out. This ended up being a challenge, because the first ear, nose, and throat doctor we hired to do this was not able to do the job. We were at an outpatient surgical center in Tampa, and I was already hooked to the saline IV and on the gurney, waiting to be wheeled into surgery. The anesthesiologist came in to meet and examine me. She was concerned with the shape of my neck and that I could not hold my head back very far. She left and, after consulting with the doctor, came back and told me that I would need to have my surgery in a hospital where the doctors would be better prepared to help if I had difficulties breathing. The doctor did not have hospital privileges for surgery.

We began another search for an otolaryngologist. Several weeks later, we found another doctor willing to do this procedure at Tampa General Hospital. This was a miracle from God, as the doctor was booked several months in advance but decided to move his schedule to accommodate the surgery. I had one eye done at a time a month apart. We ended up staying in Florida two months longer than usual. This was fine because the weather was much better than it was in Central New York in the spring. The procedure helped, and I was able to get over the infection. Prior to the surgery, I was losing my eyesight and could not drive, watch television, or read. I had to keep my eyes closed in sunlight, making it difficult to walk outside. I had to hold onto someone to keep from tripping or falling.

Later, I needed cataract surgery, and before I could have this surgery, the tubes had to come out. I went back to the same doctor who put in the tubes. Taking them out was done in his office and was a much simpler procedure. I had the tube for the left eye taken out and had the cataract surgery completed in Florida by the doctor who had discovered the cause of my infection. The next year, I had the tube taken out of the right eye and the right eye cataract removed. As of this writing, I still have some problems with dry eyes, but they are much improved. I still use several drops, plus the autologous drops and an antibiotic to keep them healthy.

Lungs:

GVHD also attacked my lungs causing scar tissue to form, impairing my breathing and the exchange or transfer of oxygen through the walls of the lungs. In addition, my lung volume has been affected. I have been able to control this with medications, including antibiotics to ward off infections and steroid inhalers to keep the airways open. Exercise also helps with this problem. Until recently, I have had my second most hated test, the pulmonary test, twice a year. The pulmonary test was always difficult for me because I had to sit in a glass, phone-booth-shaped, rectangular prism and follow commands for breathing patterns. I have had several cases of bronchitis, sinus infection, and pneumonia. I continue to have a dry cough, which is annoying, but it's much better than it has been.

In 2015, we were traveling home from Florida when I was attacked by both A and B types of influenza. During the two hours between the time that I'd started a fever and arrived at the emergency room, I had become septic. My internal organs were shutting down, and my blood pressure was forty-seven over thirty-five. I had a very difficult first night. The doctors told Wayne they were not sure I would make it through the night, but God was with me.

Just recently, I have been able to skip the pulmonary function test. Since 2015, I have not contracted the flu but have had bronchitis and other lung issues. I will always be susceptible to sinus infections and bronchitis. I continue to be careful and try not to be around sick people. This is hard, especially when it means I cannot be around the grandchildren. I try to remember that it is a small price to pay for remaining healthy, and I plan to be around them when they are healthy for many years to come.

Skin:
GVHD also took a toll on my skin. It has a mottled appearance from a rash caused by GVHD. Creams and steroids have helped this problem. In the early days after the transplant, my skin became very tight, lacking the normal elasticity of healthy skin. For several years my skin was extremely thin and would tear at the

simplest touch. Often, I would look down to see blood on my clothing, not aware I had touched anything to make me bleed. Over time, the thinness and elasticity have corrected themselves and are less of a problem. I do bruise extremely easily. When questioned about my skin, I often suggest that my tattoos are free and change daily. Some people laugh, and others look at me like I am crazy.

Joints:

In 2014, my joints started to stiffen, causing my balance to become poor. I began to stumble and fall, resulting in huge bruises and torn skin. I did not break any bones, a fact for which I am very thankful. When I returned to Roswell after being in Florida for a few months in the winter, my doctor said that if I did not get help, I would end up being like a mummy. I was confused; I did not understand all the implications this entailed. It was determined that I needed to have more steroids in heavy doses for about six months and that I needed an infusion of a chemo drug that was good for joint GVHD.

Here we went again, back to Buffalo every week for several months. I was not admitted this time but was allowed to travel back and forth two hundred miles each way to get these infusions and to have the clinic visits once a week. Thankfully, this plan did work. I became more flexible, and my balance improved, along with my skin texture.

Broken Elbow:

While we were in Florida in 2014, I was riding my beautiful new sea-green bicycle that Wayne had bought me the year before, and I crashed and broke an elbow. After allowing the swelling to go down, I had surgery, using wires and pins to replace the elbow to its rightful position. I had to give up my beautiful bicycle that I loved to ride because this was the second serious accident that required trips to the emergency room. The reason I am including this incident is that it took me seven months for my bones to heal, because I was still immunosuppressed. I was finally able to get off immunosuppression on September 3, 2018. This was ten years of taking different levels of immuno-suppressant drugs, depending on the amount of GVHD I was experiencing at the time. This is significant because some people are never able to get off these drugs completely. I tried three or four times over the years to stop taking immunosuppressant drugs, but each time the GVHD flared, and I had to increase the medicines and start the treacherous journey down again.

Jesus's arms are unseen but were there for me in every circumstance. Even now, when I am healthy and stronger, I need him every day, every hour of every day, and every minute of every hour. After I stopped taking Tacrolimus (the immuno-suppressant), which I had taken for over ten years to allow my body to adjust to having donor cells share my body, I found a wonderful freedom. This freedom included eating a lot of foods which were not on my diet previously. I remember the first green grape I ate after being on a low microbial diet for ten years. The popping sound and the succulent taste of the grape in my mouth was magnificent. After that, I began to eat salads, cold slaw, and other uncooked fruits and vegetables. For over ten years, all of my raw fruits and vegetables had to be washed in a vinegar-water solution. I could not eat berries of any kind unless they were cooked in a dessert because they were too difficult to wash.

I also found freedom socially because I am now able to be around people without continually worrying about catching germs. I am able to eat at peoples' houses and at church dinners and restaurants. I still avoid buffets, if possible.

I do not need to drink only purified water and can have ice in my drinks. I was trained to believe that ice dispensers in many restaurants are not cleaned well. I still do not have lemon in my drinks for the same reason. Often, lemons are not washed and are handled with bare hands. I am still careful to avoid sick people, but the stress of always having germs at the forefront of my mind has lessened. One of my grandsons asked me if I was a germaphobe. I told him only out of necessity. My hair has also returned to its pre-cancer thickness, which makes styling it much easier.

Depression:

I did not want to write about depression, but a friend reminded me that it was a serious part of my story and something that haunts many people dealing with long-term illnesses. About three years after the transplant, while I was actually doing very well physically, the emotional part of the illness caught up with me. I tried to deny that I was experiencing depression. In fact, I would not even say the word *depression*.

It became obvious to Wayne and Kelly that I was dealing with a mild depression, and they confronted me about the problem. I had many of the common signs of depression, such as sadness, loss of interest in things I once enjoyed, and a sense of suspicion about things that were going on around me. I did not want to leave the house unless it was absolutely necessary. Usually, when I left the house, it was for a doctor appointment.

I mostly sat on the end of the couch and worked on Sudoku and crossword puzzles. I was not interested in TV and could not enjoy reading, as I always had, because I could not focus for long periods of time.

Finally, Wayne told me that if I did not talk to the doctor about this issue, he would. At the next clinic appointment at Roswell, I talked to the NP about my feelings of depression. I think one of the reasons it was very hard for me to admit was that I'd received some faulty religious training as a child. I felt that I should be able to control depression with prayer and my faith in God.

The doctor explained to me that all the chemo I had received had caused a chemical imbalance in my brain and that depression was not something I could control without medication to help the brain chemistry to rebalance. She also asked me to identify the top five or six things that were bothering me at this time. I was able to do so and to talk these things through with Wayne, and I did visit a counselor a few times. Thankfully, my depression never got deep.

The devil, recognizing my vulnerability, began to taunt me with lies. When I was released from the hospital, I began to have the recurring thought that I was holding Wayne back from the things he wanted to accomplish after retirement from the university. Wayne worked in Brazil for a period of time, and we had originally planned to move to Brazil and teach English after we both retired. My sickness put a stop to this plan. On some level, I felt guilty about messing up our plans. This is irrational thinking, but it was very prominent in my mind. After a while, I did discuss it with Wayne, and he assured me that he did not feel as if I was holding him back. This insidious thought became rarer as time passed.

After several years, going to Buffalo was becoming more and more tedious. We decided to try to think of things to make it seem like a minivacation. One week, we decided to take our camper and camp south of Rochester at a beautiful campground there. It would put us about an hour from Buffalo and would break up the trip.

This idea was faulty from the beginning. When we arrived, the campground was a good distance from the beautiful gorge. The sites were extremely unleveled, causing the front of the camper to be much higher than the back of the camper. Wayne had some boards he used to level it, but he had to cut those in half and pile them double the original height to level the camper. This made the steps not fit properly, making entering the camper dangerous.

The first day we were there, I accidently knocked his CPAP machine off the bed. It landed on the floor and broke. Then he didn't sleep well the first night. We decided to call the company where he bought this equipment to see if they had any in stock in Syracuse. We thought we could drive back to Syracuse to get him another machine. This round trip would take most of a day. The person he talked to said that she would be going to Rochester after work for a jewelry party the next day and that she would meet us at one of the exits to carry out the transfer for the broken piece of equipment. Even though this still took up some of our free time, it did save us a long trip and worked well.

The next day, we were able to drive to the gorge and find some walking trails. The trails ran along the edge of a steep cliff. After we walked a while, I became tired and decided to sit at a picnic table while Wayne went on ahead. There were other picnic tables nearby where other people sat and chatted.

I had sat down for only a couple of minutes when this black

heaviness came over me. The heaviness came closer and became darker and heavier until it surrounded me. I heard a voice, not audible, but clear, saying over and over again, "Jump off that cliff, and your troubles will all be over. Jump off that cliff and your troubles will all be over." I am not sure how many times I heard it repeated, but it became louder and more intense each time.

Finally, from deep inside me, I heard a voice, probably my own, saying with great emphasis, "Jesus, help me!" Immediately, the darkness lifted, and it has never come back. I looked around me, and there were two young girls sitting at the picnic table next to me talking as if nothing had happened. Soon, I realized I was the only one aware of this experience. Everything around me was bright and sunny, and the view was beautiful. Not long afterward, Wayne returned, and I told him what had happened. He hugged me, and we talked about how the devil uses lies to try to destroy people at their most vulnerable times. If I had not been a child of God, I am not sure what would have happened. I have never had another experience like it, but it made an impact on me. The reason I share this is to tell people to be on guard, because the devil is a deceiver roaming the earth, seeking whom he may devour. We need to be aware of the enemy's schemes and keep our eyes open. We need to remain close to the Father, especially when we are going through our most vulnerable times.

AUTHOR'S NOTE

The reason I have written this book is not that I think I am someone special, but that God loves me just as he loves each one of you. I named the book *Unseen Arms* because at every step along this journey, I was aware of his presence. There were many nights that I went to bed and cried because I could not deal with anything more that day. I would start out crying for God's help and mercy, but I always ended up thanking him for being with me and helping me to endure one more day. I have learned so many things during this adventure, but one of the most important lessons I learned was to be thankful in all things. You might wonder how this was possible during all these trials, but in every circumstance, I was aware that I was alive and that God was with me, even carrying me. The love of a precious husband, along with my family and the prayers of many people I did not even know, helped me. I was on prayer chains up and down the East Coast and all over the country. I have only scratched the surface of all the things that have happened over these twelve years and the miracles God provided, but I think you can get the picture of what a stem cell transplant is like and of a God bigger than any of our problems. Thank you for reading my book. I pray it will encourage you.

Evelyn Hausknecht

ABOUT
THE AUTHORS

Evelyn and Wayne Hausknecht have spent most of their careers in education. Evelyn has taught different subjects and ages in public and Christian schools. Wayne, a wood engineer, helped build the largest sawmill in Brazil and has managed mills in Michigan and North Carolina.

They both enjoy motorcycle riding and rode their Harley Davidson Road King to Glacier National Park in 2006. Recently, they traded their motorcycle for a Model A truck and now enjoy going to car shows. They have two married children and six grandchildren and reside in Harrisonburg, Virginia.